# THE LEADERSHIP CHALLENGE WORKBOOK

CHAPTER 4

# THE LEADERSHIP CHALLENGE WORKBOOK

## 3RD EDITION

JAMES M. KOUZES

BARRY Z. POSNER

JOSSEY-BASS
A Wiley Imprint
www.josseybass.com

# Contents

# INTRODUCTION

**WHEN WE INTERVIEWED DON BENNETT** for our first book, he said something that we've never forgotten. Don is the first amputee to climb Mt. Rainier. That's 14,410 feet on one leg and two crutches.

"How did you make it to the top?" we asked Don.

"One hop at a time," was his instant reply.

One hop at a time. One hop at a time. One hop at a time.

When you think about it, that's how most extraordinary things are accomplished. As much as you might desire it, you simply cannot leap to the top of a mountain. You can only get there by taking it one step at a time—or, as in Don's case, one hop at a time.

Yet we sometimes find ourselves simply paralyzed by the mere scale of the challenge. We are challenged to do more with less, adapt quickly to changing circumstances, innovate on the fly, deal with extreme uncertainty, and somehow still find time for our families and friends. Sometimes it's all just too overwhelming. But so is looking up to the top of that mountain when you are at the bottom. That's why Don would tell himself, as he looked just one foot ahead, "Anybody can hop from here to there." And so he did—fourteen thousand four hundred ten times.

But Don had something else in mind when he looked up at the top of that mountain. Despite what you might have heard about why people climb mountains, it's not because they're there. When we asked Don to tell us why he wanted to be the first amputee to climb Mt. Rainier, he told us it was because he wanted to demonstrate to other disabled people that they were capable of doing more than they might have thought they could do. Don had aspirations that went beyond individual glory and success. He was the one doing the climbing, but he was not climbing just for himself. He was climbing for an entire community. He had a vision of others doing great things.

And there's another lesson we learned from Don that's directly applicable to leading others to make extraordinary things happen. We asked him, "What's the most important lesson you learned from this climb?" Without hesitation, he said, "You can't do it alone."

We produced *The Leadership Challenge Workbook* so that you can apply to your projects the leadership lessons we have learned from Don Bennett—and from the thousands of other leaders we have studied. This is a practical guide that is designed to help you use The Five Practices of Exemplary Leadership®—the model of leadership derived from, and validated by, more than thirty years of research—as a tool for planning and preparing for your next climb to the summit.

*The Leadership Challenge Workbook* is a one-hop-at-a-time guide for leaders. It's a tool that asks you to reflect on each essential element of leading and to act in ways that incrementally create forward momentum. It asks you to think beyond your personal agenda and imagine how your leadership efforts engage others' desires. And because you can't do it alone, it also helps you involve others in the planning and the doing.

## ARE YOU LEADING AT YOUR "PERSONAL BEST"?

When we began our research, we wanted to find out what practices characterize exemplary leadership, so we created a question that framed everything else. The question we asked everyone we studied was, "What did you do when you were at your 'personal best' as a leader?" We did not want to know what the most famous and the most senior leaders did. We wanted to know what leaders at *all* levels and in all contexts did.

We asked people to tell us a story about one project they led that they considered their Personal-Best Leadership Experience—an experience that set their individual standard of excellence. We collected thousands of stories of leaders performing at their peak, and we looked for actions that were consistent across all the stories.

After many years—and several thousand quantitative and qualitative analyses—we found that there are Five Practices that define exemplary leadership.

When operating at their best, leaders:

• Model the Way
• Inspire a Shared Vision
• Challenge the Process
• Enable Others to Act
• Encourage the Heart

You might already be familiar with The Five Practices from our book *The Leadership Challenge,* which describes this research in detail. Or you might know The Five Practices because you have used our 360-degree assessment instrument, the *Leadership Practices Inventory* (LPI), to further your development as a leader. In case the practices are new to you, we provide a brief overview in Chapter 2 of this workbook.

Whether you are familiar with our other work or not, we ask you to keep this in mind: When you engage in The Five Practices more frequently than you do at present, you *will* be more effective. We know from our research that those who Model, Inspire, Challenge, Enable, and Encourage more frequently significantly increase their probability of making extraordinary things happen, compared with those who do so less frequently. Exemplary leadership, in other words, is not an accident of birth or circumstance. It's a result of conscious and conscientious practice.

## PROJECTS PROVIDE THE CONTEXT

Projects are how we tend to organize work these days. Projects create the context for our goals, determine with whom we work, and set our schedules. We will be more specific in Chapter 3 about what kind of project to select, but you might start thinking now about something you are currently leading or about to lead that could benefit from the application of exemplary practices.

One important point to keep in mind is that every new project you take on provides you with an opportunity. It's an opportunity to do things the same way you have always done them, or it's an opportunity for greatness—an opportunity to achieve another personal standard of excellence. It all depends on how you approach the challenge.

No world-class athlete ever set foot on the playing field saying to himself or herself, "Well, I think I'll settle for performing at my average today." The same is true of world-class leaders. Every day is an opportunity to improve performance, and the most challenging projects are the ones that create the most opportunity. Your next project is your chance to create extraordinary results for your organization and to develop your leadership capabilities. This workbook is designed to help you plan and prepare so that you can lead at your personal best.

## WHO SHOULD USE THE LEADERSHIP CHALLENGE WORKBOOK?

This workbook is designed for anyone in a leadership role. Its purpose is to help you further your abilities to lead others in making extraordinary things happen. Whether you are in the private or public sector, an employee or a volunteer, a first-line supervisor or a senior executive, a student or a parent, you will find that this workbook applies to you. That's because leadership is not about being in a formal position. It's about action. You can grant someone the title of manager, but that does not make him or her a leader. Leadership is earned.

You get to be a leader in the eyes of others because of what you *do*. Leadership is about having the courage and spirit to move from whatever circumstances you are in to a place of making a difference in the world. This workbook is designed to help anyone who has the desire to lead and the will to make a difference. It's for anyone who is in a role that requires mobilizing others to want to struggle for shared aspirations.

## LEADERSHIP IS EVERYONE'S BUSINESS

The next time you say to yourself, "Why don't they do something about that?" look in the mirror. Ask the person you see, "Why don't *you* do something about that?" By accepting the challenge to lead, you come to realize that the only limits are those you place on yourself.

While our research has taught us many things about the practice of leadership, our interaction with the thousands of individuals we have studied has taught us something vitally important. It's driven home the lesson that leadership is everyone's business. We need more leaders today, not fewer. We need more people to accept responsibility for bringing about significant changes in what we do and how we do it. We need more people to answer the call. The world is in great need of your talents.

We believe that you are capable of developing yourself as a leader far more than tradition or mythology has ever assumed possible. Simply imagine yourself standing at the base of Mt. Rainier, and then start climbing—one hop at a time.

We wish you great joy and success on your next leadership adventure. Onward and upward!

Jim Kouzes, Orinda, California
Barry Posner, Santa Clara, California
*May 2012*

CHAPTER 1

# HOW TO USE THIS WORKBOOK

**THE BEST LEADERS** are continually learning. They see all experiences as learning opportunities. But there's one condition. Rich insights only come from reflection and analysis. Unexamined experiences yield no lessons. If you want to become a better leader, you need to study your own performance and become more conscious about the choices that you are making and how you are acting on your intentions.

The purpose of *The Leadership Challenge Workbook* is to help you become a better leader by applying The Five Practices of Exemplary Leadership® to a project of your choice. As with the learning of any new discipline, we will ask you to do some exercises that isolate specific skills. This may seem a bit artificial at first, but it's no different from any form of practice—you are not actually in the game, but you know you are improving your capacity to play the game.

# HOW THE WORKBOOK IS ORGANIZED

In Chapter 2 we've provided a summary of The Five Practices model that resulted from our thirty-plus years of research. If you've read *The Leadership Challenge* or have used the *Leadership Practices Inventory*, you may not need to review the model, but it's here if you need a reminder. If you are not already familiar with The Five Practices, read this chapter carefully—it provides the foundation for the work that you will be doing.

Chapter 3 offers some guidelines for choosing the right leadership project. To enable you to focus your work, it's essential that you select a real project to serve as the target of your reflections, applications, and actions. In Chapters 4 through 8, you'll apply The Five Practices to that project. And in Chapter 9, which you'll complete after your project is finished (or well underway), you will find questions that will help you reflect on the project's highs and lows and on what you learned—lessons you can then apply to your next Personal Best Leadership Project.

As you progress through the activities, the workbook supports your success in three ways:

1. *Reflection.* We want you to think about how you approach leadership. The questions we pose are designed to challenge your thinking and help you become more conscious about how well you engage in each of The Five Practices. Contrary to myths about leadership that assume you either have it or you don't, we know from our research that the very best leaders spend time examining what they have done as well as what they are planning to do. Call it the "mental game of leadership." The exercises in this workbook ask you to be more reflective about what your experience can teach you about leadership.

2. *Application.* We want you to apply the leadership practices and commitments to your project. To do that, we provide exercises that help put The Five Practices of Exemplary Leadership® to work. In some cases you will do this application alone. In other cases, you will go out to talk to your team members and engage them in an activity.

3. *Implications.* As a result of your reflections and applications, you will learn about yourself, your team, your organization, and your project. At the end of each chapter, we ask you to jot down the implications of what you have learned about leadership.

# GUIDELINES FOR COMPLETING THE WORKBOOK

It would be ideal if you could complete the entire workbook as a way of preparing everyone for the project—somewhat like a series of warm-up exercises before playing the game. On a practical level, that may not be possible. The way you use the workbook depends on the nature of your project and your situation. Here are some suggestions:

- If you're just starting, we recommend that you begin with Chapter 4 on Model the Way and work your way through Chapter 8 on Encourage the Heart.
- If your project has been underway for some time, we recommend that you first read through this workbook quickly, without completing all the activities. Then go back and start with those worksheets that address immediate concerns. For example, your team may have been working long hours and has not taken a break. You believe that they need some recognition and celebration. In that case, start with Chapter 8, Encourage the Heart. Or you may feel that conflicts have arisen because there is insufficient consensus around shared values. In that instance, begin with Chapter 4 on Model the Way. However, make sure you address all of The Five Practices and complete all the activities as soon as you can. They are designed to improve the way you lead.
- You may find that you have already completed some of the activities that are in this workbook. For instance, you and your team may have spent a lot of time identifying and agreeing upon your shared values. If you have already done something equivalent to what's in this workbook, then just pause long enough to make sure you are comfortable with what you have done and do not need to revisit it. Then move on to the next activity.
- You may decide that you want to start with a particular chapter—say Chapter 7 instead of Chapter 4—because you think the activities in that chapter are more important to your team right now. Or you may find that some questions are richer and more useful to you than others. That's okay with us. Start with the practice that most needs your attention. We encourage you to proceed through this book in whatever way resonates for you.
- No matter how you use the workbook, however, we urge you not to skip over any of the leadership practices.

At times you may find yourself saying, "I don't know." For example, we are going to ask, "Who's on your project team?" Your answer today may be, "I don't know. The team members haven't been selected yet." That's a perfectly acceptable response. If you are not ready to answer a question or complete an activity, set the workbook aside and do what you need to do so that you can respond or engage in action, or simply move on to the next question or activity and come back when you are ready. What's important is·that you come back to everything that you skip.

Becoming a better leader requires learning and doing something in each of The Five Practices. You may be better at some than others, but you still have to develop your capacity to execute in all of them. It's like participating in a pentathlon. You can't opt out of any of the five events if you want to enter. You may feel that you are better prepared for some of the events than for others, but you must still participate in all five.

# CHAPTER 2

# THE FIVE PRACTICES OF EXEMPLARY LEADERSHIP

**WE'VE BEEN CONDUCTING INTENSIVE RESEARCH** on leadership since 1982. During that entire time, in selecting the people to interview and survey we have consistently chosen not to focus on famous people in positions of power who make headlines. Instead, we've always wanted to know what the vast majority of leaders do—those ordinary people who make extraordinary things happen in organizations. We have concentrated our research on everyday people who lead project teams, manage departments, administer schools, organize community groups, and volunteer for student and civic organizations.

To conduct our research, we've asked thousands of people, in writing and in interviews, to tell us about their Personal-Best Leadership Experiences. Each person was asked to select a project, program, or significant event that represented a time he or she believed represented his or her own "best practices" leadership experience—the one he or she personally recalled when thinking about a peak leadership performance.

Despite the differences in people's individual stories, the Personal-Best Leadership Experiences that we read and listened to revealed similar patterns of action. We found that when leaders are at their personal best, they engage in The Five Practices of Exemplary Leadership®. They:

- Model the Way
- Inspire a Shared Vision
- Challenge the Process
- Enable Others to Act
- Encourage the Heart

Let's take a brief look at each of these practices before you apply them to your project.

# MODEL THE WAY

Titles are granted, but it's your behavior that wins you respect. If you want to gain commitment and achieve the highest standards, you must be a model of the behavior that you expect of others.

To model effectively, you must first believe in something. As a leader, you are supposed to stand up for your beliefs, so you had better have some beliefs to stand up for. The first commitment you must make, then, is to *clarify values by finding your voice and affirming shared values* and then expressing them in a style that is authentically your own.

Eloquent speeches about your personal values are not nearly enough. Your deeds are far more important than your words when expressing how serious you are about what you say, and your words and deeds must be consistent. Exemplary *leaders set the example by aligning actions with shared values.* They go first. You go first by setting the example through daily actions that demonstrate you are deeply committed to your beliefs. And you must take the actions necessary to build consensus around shared values. You can't impose your values on others, no matter how hard you try or how much power you have. Unless values are shared among all those who work together, intense commitment is impossible. What you get is simply compliance.

The personal-best projects were all distinguished by relentless effort, steadfastness, competence, and attention to detail. We were struck by how the actions leaders took to set the example were often simple things. Sure, leaders had operational and strategic plans, but the actions they described were all the day-to-day things they did to practice what they preached.

You set the example by spending time with someone, by working side-by-side with colleagues, by telling stories that make the values come alive, by being highly visible during times of uncertainty, and by asking questions to help people to think about values and priorities. Modeling the way is essentially about earning the right and the respect to lead through direct individual involvement and action. People have to believe in the messenger or they won't pay attention to the message. They first follow the person, then the plan.

## INSPIRE A SHARED VISION

In describing their Personal-Best Leadership Experiences, people recounted times when they imagined an exciting, highly attractive future for their organization. They had visions and dreams of what could be. They had absolute and total personal belief in those dreams, and they were confident in their abilities to make extraordinary things happen. Every organization, every social movement, begins with a dream.

Leaders *envision the future by imagining exciting and ennobling possibilities.* They gaze across the horizon of time, imagining the attractive opportunities that are in store once they and their constituents arrive at the final destination. Leaders have a desire to make something happen, to change how things are, to create something that no one else has ever created before.

In some ways, leaders live their lives backward. They see pictures in their minds' eyes of what the results will look like even before they have started their projects, much as an architect draws a blueprint or an engineer builds a model. Their clear image of the future pulls them forward. Yet a vision seen only by a leader is insufficient to create an organized movement or a significant change in an organization. A person with no constituents is not a leader, and people do not follow until they accept a vision as their own. Leaders cannot command commitment; they can only inspire it. Leaders *enlist others in a common vision by appealing to shared aspirations.*

To enlist people in a vision, as a leader you must know your constituents and be able to relate to them in ways that energize and uplift them. People must believe that their leaders understand their needs and have their interests at heart. Only through an intimate knowledge of their dreams, hopes, aspirations, visions, and values are you able to enlist support. Leadership is a dialogue, not a monologue.

Leaders breathe life into the hopes and dreams of others and enable them to see the exciting possibilities that the future holds. Leaders forge unity of purpose by showing constituents how the dream is for the common good. You cannot ignite the flame of passion in others if you cannot express enthusiasm for the compelling vision of the group. You must communicate your passion through vivid language and expressive style.

Without exception, the leaders we have studied reported that they were incredibly enthusiastic about their personal-best projects. Their own excitement was catching; it spread from leader to constituents. Their belief in and commitment to the vision were the sparks that ignited the flame of inspiration.

## CHALLENGE THE PROCESS

Leaders venture out. The individuals we studied did not sit idly by waiting for fate to smile upon them. While "luck" or "being in the right place at the right time" may play a role in the specific opportunities leaders embrace, those who lead others to greatness seek and accept challenge.

Every single Personal-Best Leadership Experience we collected involved some kind of challenge. The challenge may have been developing an innovative new product, coming up with a cutting-edge service, shaping a groundbreaking piece of legislation, spearheading an invigorating campaign to get adolescents to join an environmental program, leading a revolutionary turnaround of a bureaucratic military program, or starting up a new plant or business. Whatever the challenge, all the cases involved a change from the status quo. Not onc person claimed to have done his or her personal best by keeping things the same. All leaders break the "business-as-usual" mold.

Leaders are pioneers—people who are willing to step out into the unknown. They *search for opportunities by seizing the initiative and by looking outward for innovative ways to improve.* But it's impossible for you, or for any leader, to be the only creator or originator of new products, services, or processes. Product and service innovations tend to come from customers, clients, vendors, people in the labs, and people on the front lines, while process innovations tend to come from the people doing the work. Your primary contribution to the search for opportunities is in the recognition of good ideas, the support of those ideas, and the willingness to challenge the system in order to get new products, processes, services, and systems adopted.

Leaders know well that innovation and change require them to *experiment and take risks by constantly generating small wins and learning from experience.* Incremental steps and little victories piled on top of each other build enough confidence to meet even the biggest challenges. By building incrementally, you strengthen commitment to the long-term future. Yet not everyone is equally comfortable with risk and uncertainty. You also must pay attention to the capacity of your constituents to take control of challenging situations and become fully committed to change.

Yet even the most prepared and skilled people never succeed at 100 percent of what they do. This is even truer when they are taking big risks and experimenting with new, untried concepts and methods. Risk and experimentation are always accompanied by mistakes and failure. The key that unlocks the door to opportunity is learning. Great leaders are great learners. You must create a climate in which people can learn from their failures as well as their successes.

## ENABLE OTHERS TO ACT

Grand dreams do not become significant realities through the actions of a single leader. Leadership is a team effort. After reviewing thousands of Personal-Best Leadership Experiences, we developed a simple test to detect whether someone is on the road to becoming a leader. They get further ahead the more they use the word *we* rather than *I*.

Exemplary leaders Enable Others to Act. They *foster collaboration by building trust and facilitating relationships.* This sense of teamwork goes far beyond a few direct reports or close confidants. In today's virtual organizations, cooperation cannot be restricted to a small group of loyalists; it must include peers, managers, customers and clients, suppliers, citizens—all those who have a stake in the vision. You have to involve, in some way, everyone who must live with the results, and you must make it possible for others to do good work.

Leaders also know that no one does his or her best when feeling weak, incompetent, or alienated; they know that those who are expected to produce the results must feel a sense of personal power and ownership. Leaders work to *strengthen others by increasing self-determination and developing competence.* They enable people to deliver on the promises they make. They know that you can't hoard the power you have as a leader; you must give it away. When you trust others and give them more discretion, authority, and information, they are much more likely to use their energies to produce extraordinary results.

In the cases we analyzed, leaders proudly discussed teamwork, trust, and empowerment as essential elements of their efforts. A leader's ability to Enable Others to Act is essential. Constituents neither perform at their best nor stick around for very long if their leader makes them weak, dependent, or alienated. When you make someone feel strong and capable—as if he or she can do more than he or she ever thought possible—that person will give all and exceed your own expectations. When leadership is a relationship, founded on trust and confidence, people take risks, make changes, and keep organizations and movements alive.

## ENCOURAGE THE HEART

The climb to the top is arduous and long. People become exhausted, frustrated, and disenchanted. They are often tempted to give up. Leaders Encourage the Heart of their constituents to carry on. Genuine acts of caring uplift the spirits and draw people forward. No one likes to be taken for granted.

Encouragement can come from dramatic gestures or simple actions. It's part of the leader's job to *recognize contributions by showing appreciation for individual excellence.* In the cases we collected, there were thousands of examples of individual recognition. We've heard and seen everything, including marching bands, costumed skits, "This Is Your Life" imitations, as well as T-shirts, note cards, personal thank-you's, and a host of other awards. Leaders also *celebrate the values and victories by creating a spirit of community.* Celebrations are not about fun and games, although there is a lot of fun and there are a lot of games when you Encourage the Hearts of your constituents. Neither are they about pretentious ceremonies designed to create a phony sense of camaraderie. When people observe a charlatan making noisy affectations, they turn away in disgust. Encouragement is curiously serious business. It's how leaders visibly and behaviorally link rewards with performance.

When striving to raise quality, recover from disaster, start up a new service, or make dramatic change of any kind, leaders make sure people see the benefit of behavior that's aligned with cherished values, including reminders that success is a function of everyone's efforts and achieved through working together as a team. Leaders also know that celebrations and rituals, when done with authenticity and from the heart, build a strong sense of collective identity and community spirit that can carry a group through extraordinary tough times.

## THE FIVE PRACTICES AND TEN COMMITMENTS OF LEADERSHIP

Embedded in The Five Practices of Exemplary Leadership® are behaviors that can serve as the basis for learning to lead. We call these The Ten Commitments of Leadership. The Five Practices and The Ten Commitments serve as the structure for this workbook, and as the foundation that supports the activities in this workbook. We'll apply them to your project in the chapters that follow.

Take a look at the following page for a summary of The Five Practices and The Ten Commitments. They're what leaders use to make extraordinary things happen in organizations. Let them be your guide on your journey to success.

## TABLE 2.1 THE FIVE PRACTICES AND TEN COMMITMENTS OF EXEMPLARY LEADERSHIP

| Practice | | Commitments |
|---|---|---|
| **Model the Way** | | 1. Clarify values by finding your voice and affirming shared values. |
| | | 2. Set the example by aligning actions with shared values. |
| **Inspire a Shared Vision** | | 3. Envision the future by imagining exciting and ennobling possibilities. |
| | | 4. Enlist others in a common vision by appealing to shared aspirations. |
| **Challenge the Process** | | 5. Search for opportunities by seizing the initiative and by looking outward for innovative ways to improve. |
| | | 6. Experiment and take risks by constantly generating small wins and learning from experience. |
| **Enable Others to Act** | | 7. Foster collaboration by building trust and facilitating relationships. |
| | | 8. Strengthen others by increasing self-determination and developing competence. |
| **Encourage the Heart** | | 9. Recognize contributions by showing appreciation for individual excellence. |
| | | 10. Celebrate the values and victories by creating a spirit of community. |

# CHAPTER 3

# SELECTING YOUR PERSONAL-BEST LEADERSHIP PROJECT

**IN TODAY'S ORGANIZATIONS THE PROJECT** is the most common way people organize their efforts. Publishing this workbook is a project. Getting a new product launched is a project. Making a movie is a project. Implementing a quality improvement process is a project. Remodeling your house is a project. Putting on this year's management conference is a project. Raising funds for a new homeless shelter is a project. Some projects are small projects within big projects. And, usually, one project leads to another. So we'd like you to begin *The Leadership Challenge Workbook* process by selecting a real-world leadership project as the framework for applying The Five Practices.

Your leadership project should meet these six basic criteria:

- *The project is about changing business as usual.* Although there are some projects about keeping things the same, those are not leadership projects. Select a project that involves starting something new or making meaningful changes in how something is being done or both.

- *You're the leader.* You may be a contributor on a number of projects, but for purposes of this workbook, select one for which you are leading the effort. You might be the leader because you are the manager, and it's part of your job, or because you have been selected to lead by your manager. You might be the leader because you've been elected by the team or because you have volunteered for the role. Whatever is the case, select a project for which you are the leader.

- *The project has an identifiable starting and stopping place.* While there may be other things going on at the same time, and while other things may continue after it's over, the project needs a deadline.

- *The project has a specific objective that it's intended to accomplish.* At the end of the project, a new product will have been successfully released, a new system successfully installed, the top of a mountain successfully reached. Whatever the objective, there will be something at the conclusion of the project that everyone can point to and say, "We did it!"

- *The project involves other people.* There are projects you might do by yourself, but you cannot do a leadership project by yourself. It takes a team to make extraordinary things happen in organizations.

- *The project is about to start or has just started.* While you should seek to improve your leadership in whatever you do, for purposes of this activity you should select something that is not too far along in the process. You will find this workbook more useful if you pick a project that's just getting underway or will soon launch.

Here are some examples of projects that are candidates for the process in this workbook:

- You are trying to institute a new system or process—a new customer resource management system, for instance—and expect to face some resistance.

- You have been assigned to turn around a factory that's had a history of poor labor-management relations.

- You have volunteered to lead a local environmental clean-up campaign.

- You are heading a team responsible for instituting a new teacher development program.

- You are taking over a project that got off track, and you need to restart it and still make the original deadline.

- You need to grow business this quarter despite a downturn in the economy and a cut in your budget.
- You are creating a new event: a program, publication, association, or something no one has ever done before.
- You are opening a new territory or launching a new product.

In addition to the six criteria we've listed, there's one other thing you should keep in mind. This is a Personal-Best Leadership Project, so you're setting out to perform at your highest levels. Select a project that represents *a significant challenge to you*. We know from our research that challenge is the opportunity for greatness. People are much more likely to do their best when they're stretched to exceed what they've done before. New assignments, turnarounds, cross-cultural experiences, and the like are good candidates for projects that offer that kind of opportunity. Only you can determine what's a stretch for you, but for the purposes of this process do not select something that's comfortable and easy.

Now—use the Personal-Best Leadership Project worksheet that begins on the next page to describe your project. In the next five chapters, you will explore The Five Practices of Exemplary Leadership in turn, with a focus on expanding and enhancing your own leadership practices as you lead this project. We believe that the questions and activities on those pages will be instrumental in your achieving a personal best.

# MY PERSONAL-BEST LEADERSHIP PROJECT

Take a few minutes to reflect on your leadership role—whether formal or informal, appointed, selected, or self-initiated—and the various projects (impending or just initiated) that meet the criteria outlined in this chapter. Your project does not have to be a project at the office. Remember what we said in the beginning: leadership is everyone's business. Your project can be one that involves your community, religious organization, professional or volunteer association, or your work. You will find that you can use this workbook for all kinds of change initiatives.

Identify the project you have selected to work through in this workbook.

_____

_____

_____

_____

_____

Now look at what you know so far about this project. (Remember, you may not be able to answer all of these questions, so respond to what you can and come back to this section when you can complete the rest.)

As far as they've been determined, what are the *project goals*?

_____

_____

_____

_____

_____

What's the *time frame*?

_____

_____

What's the *budget*?

_____

_____

_____

What are the *challenges* that you face in leading this project? For example:

- Funding is limited due to an economic downturn.
- The constituents are apathetic about, or even resistant to, change.
- Team members have great technical skills, but they lack skills in collaboration.
- The last new product or service was not well-received, and there's pressure to make this one a winner.
- There's not a lot of upper management support for this initiative.

Challenges for leading this project:

_____

_____

_____

_____

_____

_____

_____

Who's on the immediate *project team*? Include titles, positions, and roles, as well as what you know about each person that's relevant to the project's success. For example:

- Mario—Human resources representative—staff resource to team on HR issues; strengths include people skills and intimate knowledge of who's who in organization.

- Jean—Senior software engineer—responsible for supervising technical aspects of project; strong technical skills, very credible with engineers, highly creative and innovative thinker.
- Tyrone—Technical writer—doing much of the text for manuals; new to organization, but very talented at making technical material readable for a non-technical audience.

Team member: _____

_____

Team member: _____

_____

Team member: _____

_____

Team member: _____

_____

Team member: _____

_____

Team member: _____

_____

Team member: _____

_____

Team member: _____

_____

If you have more than eight team members, photocopy this page or continue on another sheet of paper.

What other possible team members should you consider? What other stakeholders have a vested interest in the success of the project? A stakeholder might be a peer whose support you need, your boss or another manager in your organization, a vendor, or a key customer or client who may be using what you produce as a result of the project. What criteria will each stakeholder use to measure success?

Examples:

- Stakeholder or stakeholder group: *Rick, HR Manager*
- Criteria for success: *Morale is high; people report being highly satisfied with the others on the team; turnover is low*
- Stakeholder or stakeholder group: *Caroline, CFO*
- Criteria for success: *Project is within budget; financial reporting is on time*
- Stakeholder or stakeholder group: *Jaime, clinical services director*
- Criteria for success: *State of the technology and processes are deployed; results in a journal article*

Stakeholder or stakeholder group: _____
Criteria for success:

_____

_____

Stakeholder or stakeholder group: _____
Criteria for success:

_____

_____

Stakeholder or stakeholder group: _____
Criteria for success:

_____

_____

Stakeholder or stakeholder group: _____
Criteria for success:

_____

_____

Stakeholder or stakeholder group: _____
Criteria for success:

_____

_____

If you have more than five key stakeholders, photocopy this page or continue on another sheet of paper.

What are your current feelings regarding this project? List several words that describe those feelings, such as *excitement, dread, panic, anticipation,* and so forth.

_____

_____

_____

What aspects of this project do you expect to be frustrating or difficult? List the specific aspects of this undertaking that are most challenging.

_____

_____

_____

Why is this project important . . .

To you?

_____

_____

_____

_____

To your organization?

_____

_____

_____

_____

To others (for example, the community, stockholders, other departments, colleagues, and others)?

_____

_____

_____

_____

_____

_____

_____

_____

# CHAPTER 4

# MODEL THE WAY

**THE FIRST STEP YOU MUST TAKE ALONG THE PATH** to becoming an exemplary leader is to discover your personal values and beliefs. You must define a set of principles that guide your decisions and actions and find a way to express them in your own words, not in someone else's. You must find your voice.

Yet leaders don't just speak for themselves. They also speak for their team and organization. Therefore, you must understand and appreciate the values of your constituents and find a way to affirm shared values. This way, you give people reasons to care, not simply orders to follow.

Finally, leaders stand up for their beliefs. They practice what they preach. They show others by their actions that they live by the values they profess. They also ensure that others adhere to the values that have been agreed upon. It is consistency between words and actions that builds credibility.

To Model the Way, you *clarify values* by finding your voice and affirming shared values and *set the example* by aligning personal actions with shared values.

Here are some examples from the personal-best cases we've collected of how leaders Model the Way:

*The manager of a manufacturing facility* saw that housekeeping conditions around the site didn't meet the plant's vision of being a "World Class Plant." He painted the words "World Class Plant" on a two-gallon plastic bucket and began walking around every day picking up trash. Word spread quickly and it didn't take long for more buckets to appear. The process he started by his visible example soon became the norm and generated lots of new ideas about how they could make the job of cleaning the plant easier.

*A senior district manager in a telecommunications company* began her new job assignment by taking her management team on a retreat. The purpose of the retreat was to develop a set of principles that would serve as a guide for all team members. She began by sharing her personal values and then engaging the team in a discussion of their personal values. At the retreat the team developed a set of common values and made a commitment to discuss them with all their direct reports after the meeting.

*The president of a chain of neighborhood convenience stores* does not just talk about the importance of employee satisfaction and work/family balance. On important national holidays, he and other corporate office staff members work in the stores so that employees can spend time with their families.

*The division manager of an electric and gas utility* works diligently to demonstrate the importance of customers. She makes a point every day of bringing up customers in her daily interactions with other employees. The first agenda item in her staff meetings is always customer satisfaction.

*The new superintendent of a major inner-city school system* inherited a district that, like many, faced a huge budget deficit, had a majority of students with below-average standardized test scores, enrolled a highly diverse student body, and had a host of other problems. He wanted to demonstrate his commitment to improvement in a highly visible manner. On the first day of school he held a district-wide rally at a large stadium near downtown. It was attended by students, teachers, and administrators from all over the district. He wrote a personal pledge to all, and he had a local superior court judge administer this oath to him before the entire audience. He then repeated this act every year he was superintendent.

## OBJECTIVES

As a result of completing the worksheets in this chapter you will be better able to:

- Clearly articulate your personal values to the members of your project team
- Engage your team members in a discussion of their values
- Build consensus on shared values
- Align your leadership actions with the shared values

# Reflect & Apply

## REFLECTION 1

Think back over the last several years and recall the projects you have been a part of, whether you were the leader or not. Identify two or three that were the most meaningful, energizing, enriching, and fun for you. What would you say characterized these experiences? What made them meaningful, energizing, enriching, and fun? What made you want to continue to be part of them? Make a list of these attributes.

_____

_____

_____

_____

_____

_____

_____

What do the attributes you listed above say about what you value in the way projects are conducted? For example, you might say, "One of the things that I liked most about the project was the chance to work with some really talented people on a project that was really cutting-edge. This tells me that 'teamwork and collaboration,' 'innovation,' and 'intelligence' are important values to me." Another way of asking this question is: What values and what actions are important to you in creating a climate in which you feel both happy and successful?

_____

_____

_____

_____

# REFLECTION 2

Imagine that it's one year after your project was successfully concluded. You overhear several people talking about the legacy you've left as a result of how the project was handled. What two or three things do you hope to hear them say?

_____

_____

_____

What are you already doing to help create this legacy?

_____

_____

_____

_____

What do you need to start doing to create this legacy?

_____

_____

_____

_____

_____

_____

_____

_____

_____

# APPLICATION 1

## Clarify Your Values

The late Milton Rokeach, one of the leading scholars and researchers in the field of human values, referred to a value as an enduring belief about the way things should be done or about the ends we desire. Values are principles that are intrinsically important to us, and it's unlikely that we will easily change them.

Your values are the underlying principles that guide your decisions. It's absolutely essential that you be clear and mindful of the values that guide your actions, because your personal credibility depends on it. So we'll start with clarifying the values that you believe should guide your actions in this project.

### *Identify Your Values*

For this project, which values are most important to its successful completion? What principles do you want everyone to understand and hold as priorities? Review the list we offer here of some commonly held values. On the blank lines at the end of the list, add any values that you think are missing. Then put check marks next to the five values that you feel are most important in the success of your project.

| | | |
|---|---|---|
| ☐ Achievement/Success | ☐ Dependability | ☐ Happiness |
| ☐ Autonomy | ☐ Discipline | ☐ Harmony |
| ☐ Beauty | ☐ Diversity | ☐ Health |
| ☐ Challenge | ☐ Effectiveness | ☐ Honesty/Integrity |
| ☐ Communication | ☐ Empathy | ☐ Hope |
| ☐ Competence | ☐ Equality | ☐ Humor |
| ☐ Competition | ☐ Family | ☐ Independence |
| ☐ Courage | ☐ Flexibility | ☐ Innovation |
| ☐ Creativity | ☐ Friendship | ☐ Intelligence |
| ☐ Curiosity | ☐ Freedom | ☐ Love/Affection |
| ☐ Decisiveness | ☐ Growth | ☐ Loyalty |

- ☐ Open-Mindedness
- ☐ Patience
- ☐ Power
- ☐ Productivity
- ☐ Prosperity/Wealth
- ☐ Quality
- ☐ Recognition

- ☐ Respect
- ☐ Risk Taking
- ☐ Security
- ☐ Service
- ☐ Simplicity
- ☐ Spirituality/Faith
- ☐ Strength

- ☐ Teamwork
- ☐ Trust
- ☐ Truth
- ☐ Variety
- ☐ Wisdom
- ☐ _____
- ☐ _____

## *Set Your Priorities*

Because you hold many values, at times some of them will be in conflict with others. For example, let's say you identify a new technology that can increase your department's productivity, but it will also lead to some layoffs. In your decision process, you are likely to weigh such values as productivity and profitability against, say, loyalty, security, and respect for employees' family needs. This kind of conflict cannot be avoided. It's important to achieve a greater understanding of your priorities so you are better able to resolve the inevitable conflicts.

To help you be clearer about the priorities of your values, list the five values you selected on the lines below. Then distribute a total of 100 points among the five. Be sure to assign a numerical value to each of the priorities—if you decide not to assign a numerical value to a priority, it should not be on your list.

*Value*       *Points*

_____    ____

_____    ____

_____    ____

_____    ____

_____    ____

Total Points: 100

Now what does this activity tell you about what you feel is most important?

_____

_____

_____

_____

_____

_____

_____

_____

# APPLICATION 2

## Check the Fit

If your leadership project is inside a formal organization, there may be an expressed set of organizational values that everyone is expected to adhere to. We know from our research that it is not possible to be fully committed to the organization if your personal values conflict with the organization's values. So take a moment to do a fitness check.

• Does your organization have a published set of values? If yes, take them out and look at them. If not, there may be a set of values that's lived out anyway. For instance, you may observe that whenever something needs to be done, individuals go off to their own cubicles or offices and work alone, implying that this organization values individual achievement as compared to teamwork and collaboration. Another clue that this is a value is that all awards and recognitions are given to individuals and not to groups.

• What are values in your organization?

_____

_____

_____

_____

• If you're not clear about your organization's values, what can you do to gain that clarity?

_____

_____

_____

_____

- Now think about how your personal values relate to the organization's values. Where is there alignment? Where do your values and the organization's appear to conflict?

| Personal Value | Organization's Value | Alignment? (Yes/No) |
| --- | --- | --- |
| _____ | _____ | _____ |
| _____ | _____ | _____ |
| _____ | _____ | _____ |
| _____ | _____ | _____ |
| _____ | _____ | _____ |
| _____ | _____ | _____ |

If there appears to be alignment between your values and the organization's values, move on to the next application exercise. If not, determine how you are going to resolve the conflict.

One way to find better fit between your personal values and those of the organization is to engage in a dialogue with your manager about the situation. Another way is to talk it over with your family or a close colleague. Sometimes we find that the conflict is a result of a lack of clarity, and sometimes it's because you can't figure out how to meet your needs and the organization's at the same time. Whatever the root cause, you must address the conflict. You cannot be a good role model of what the organization values if you are not fully on board with it.

☐ There is alignment. (Move on.)
☐ There are conflicts. I will do the following to resolve them:

_____

_____

_____

_____

_____

# APPLICATION 3

## Build and Affirm Shared Values

When you're an individual contributor working alone, you might be able to use your personal values as a guide. But when you are the leader, other folks' values need to be considered if they are going to be committed. Because we know from our research that commitment flows from a strong sense that personal values are clear and shared, it's important to discuss values at the beginning of a project. If you have not done so already, now is the time to talk to your team about values.

---

# NOTE

If you have not yet assembled your team, come back and do this activity after you have.

---

Here's what we suggest that you do.

- Gather the most immediate members of your project team together for a meeting. (It would be great if you could do this in a retreat setting.) Let people know ahead of time that you are coming together to talk about the principles that will guide your decisions and actions as you move forward.

- During the meeting, have every individual complete Application 1 (pages 35 through 37)—the same one you used to clarify your own values. (You have our permission to reproduce the Application 1: Clarify Values worksheet for each team member.) Have them select the values they think are important. Tell them you have already done this, and you now want them to do the same.

- After everyone has completed the task, be the first to communicate the values on your list. Tell them about any conflicts and tensions you might have had during the process. By doing this you are already setting the example of what you expect of people, and you are also working to build your own personal credibility. Ask everyone to share the values on their lists.

• Once everyone has had the chance to communicate personal values, look for the values that team members hold in common. What values appear on everyone's list? What values do a majority of the group hold? Where are there conflicts? For example, do a majority of the team members value teamwork and collaboration, but a few value individualism and independence more? Discuss how these kinds of tensions can be resolved.

• As a final step, produce a one-page "team credo" articulating the principles that will guide all of you during the project. Post this credo prominently so that the values are visible as a reference to guide everyone's actions and decisions.

# APPLICATION 4

## Align Your Actions with Shared Values

"Actions speak louder than words" is a common refrain. So it is with your leadership actions. The extent to which your actions are consistent with your words determines your personal credibility. And the extent to which your actions are consistent with shared values determines your *leadership* credibility. Now that you have a clearer sense of shared values, you need to make sure there's alignment between words and deeds.

As project leader, what can you do to demonstrate the importance of the shared values to the team members, to colleagues, and to management? Brainstorm two or three actions you can take to show your commitment to each value. Actions might include how you spend your time, how you deal with critical incidents, the stories you tell, or the way you ask questions and express yourself.

- *How you spend your time.* The actual allocation of your time to key values sends a message. For example, if creativity is on the list of principles important to the project, then you need to spend some of your own time in pursuit of creativity. It might be by visiting a product design firm to see how they stimulate creativity, or it might be by participating in a team brainstorming session.

  Where and how do you need to spend your time?

  _____

  _____

  _____

  _____

  _____

- *How you deal with critical incidents.* The way you handle specific important events or episodes in times of stress and challenge can be opportunities for demonstrating commitment to a value. They are what we call "teachable moments." For instance, let's say your team values collaboration, but there's one very bright member of the group who consistently comes unprepared to meetings. When you confront him, he says that he doesn't need to prepare because his performance is better than that of the other members of the team. How you handle this "lone wolf" will send a strong message about whether teamwork is for everyone, or for everyone except this talented individualist. If you are true to the teamwork value, you will be clear with this individual that you expect him to come prepared like everyone else. There are no exceptions, regardless of how many sales he makes. You will then set some very specific next steps for meeting with this individual to monitor his progress and to offer coaching if needed.

What are some ways you can prepare yourself to handle potential critical incidents?

_____

_____

_____

_____

_____

_____

_____

_____

- *Telling stories about exemplary actions by others.* We are all fond of telling stories, and telling stories about a member of the team who does something to live out one of the project values is a very useful way to demonstrate that you are paying attention to what's going on.

Who has done something recently to exemplify a shared value? Where and when can you tell the story about what this person did so that others can learn from it?

## NOTE

If you are just beginning your project, you might have to come back and answer this question later.

_____

_____

_____

_____

_____

- *Choose your language carefully and ask questions that probe key values.* Words are very powerful, and you need to choose them carefully. Let's say your team values service to others, but the language you and others use is all about "What's in it for me?" After hearing this over and over, what do you think people will assume is important?

Similarly, the questions you ask can stimulate action in a particular direction. If you want people to be constantly innovative, try asking something like this on a regular basis: "What have you done in the last week to improve so that you're better this week than you were seven days ago?"

What key words do you want to make sure you use to signal commitment to your core values? What words do you want to make sure you avoid and discourage? What questions can you ask to stimulate people to align their thoughts and actions around the core values?

*Key Words to Use*

_____

_____

_____

*Key Words to Avoid*

_____

_____

_____


*Questions to Ask*

_____

_____

_____

_____

# APPLICATION 5

## Select Actions

Review your responses to the questions above on your use of time, critical incidents, stories, and language. For each of your top three project values, select at least one action from the options you generated above that you can take to personally demonstrate each of your project's shared values. If you do not have an action for each shared value, then make a note of it so that you come back to it later.

*Value*                  *Actions I'll Take Personally*

_____          _____

_____          _____

_____          _____

_____          _____

_____          _____

_____          _____

## IMPLICATIONS

What have you learned about yourself as a leader from the activities in this chapter?

_____

_____

_____

_____

_____

_____

_____

_____

Based on your experience with these application exercises, what do you need to do in order to improve how you Model the Way during this project?

_____

_____

_____

_____

_____

CHAPTER 5

# INSPIRE A SHARED VISION

**LEADERS LOOK FORWARD TO THE FUTURE.** They hold in their minds visions and ideas of what can be. They have a sense of what is uniquely possible if everyone works together for a common purpose.

But visions seen only by the leaders are not enough to make extraordinary things happen. They must help others to see the exciting future possibilities and communicate hopes and dreams so that others clearly understand and share them as their own. Leaders show other people how their values and interests will be served by a long-term vision of the future. With their energy and optimism, through strong appeals and quiet persuasion, they develop enthusiastic supporters.

To Inspire a Shared Vision, you *envision the future* by imagining exciting and ennobling possibilities, and you *enlist others* in a common vision by appealing to shared aspirations.

## WHAT IS A VISION?

We define vision as an ideal and unique image of the future for the common good. To be able to inspire others you need to be able to state what's unique and distinctive about your vision of the future. You need to be able to describe it so that people can picture it in their own minds—"Oh, I see what you're talking about!" And you need to be able to talk about the future, not just the present, in a way that is appealing to a large number of people. Your vision may be compelling to you, but if it's not attractive to others they will not move toward it.

Here are examples from our personal-best cases of actions that helped some leaders Inspire a Shared Vision.

> *An insurance executive* assigned each of her dozen team members three different magazines and newspapers to read. Some were popular magazines, and others were industry-related. She wanted the reading to be diverse, so the publications covered the gamut from popular music to science and technology. The task of each reader was to look for articles that had implications for their business in the future and then to write one-page summaries of the trends and their implications for the business. Each quarter the team members would meet to discuss their work and look for themes. This process of continually scanning the horizon for emerging trends helped the team stay ahead of the curve.

> *A forest ranger* was heading up a reforestation project after a major fire. He described the work as a "great cause." He continually talked about how this project was about helping future generations, making life better for others in the long run. It was something they were doing for their grandchildren and great-grandchildren.

*The president of a financial services company* needed to get his organization on board with a new range of services that were a break from the tradition of the company. At the annual management off-site retreat, everyone was asked to write down one dream he or she had for the future and then paint it onto a piece of ceramic tile. That evening, the managers stood around a bonfire, read what they had written, and then placed the painted ceramic tiles in the fire. The next morning when they arrived in the meeting room they saw a large multi-media art piece that had been constructed from their tiles. The image was of a man looking through a telescope into the future. This piece was hung in the company conference room and, of course, caused folks who saw it to ask, "What's that?" It became a perfect opportunity to talk about a shared vision of the future.

*The community outreach program coordinator of a state university* wanted to provide an educational and service opportunity for students to engage with issues and people who were unfamiliar to them. He traveled to San Francisco with a group of students for the school's first-ever "alternative" spring break. This group slept on the floor of a San Francisco church and worked at local homeless shelters. Each night they cooked dinner together and discussed the day's events as they ate. After dinner they gathered to participate in team-building exercises, discuss social issues related to their service experiences, write in the group's journal, and prepare for the next day's work. His fondest wish for the project was for students to return to campus with a new sense of passion and commitment to social justice.

*A registered nurse in her new role as unit leader of a hospital intensive care/ cardiac care unit* was part of a team opening a new state-of-the-art facility. She found ways to fully engage her colleagues in that exciting opportunity by turning to the local Native American culture to create a team mascot and a "passport" that included a map of the new site and a checklist for working safely in the new environment. Those innovations, plus a mock patient setup room where the staff could practice using the new technology and equipment hands-on, brought the team's vision to life and lessened the anxiety on moving day.

## OBJECTIVES

As a result of completing the worksheets in this chapter you will be better able to:

*   Articulate your personal vision of the future to the members of your project team
*   Engage your team members in a dialogue about their hopes, dreams, and aspirations
*   Enlist others in a common vision
*   Communicate the common vision in an attractive, appealing way

# Reflect & Apply

## REFLECTION 1

Make a list of four or five experiences from your past that have been "turning points" for you—experiences that have truly influenced the direction you have taken in your life. These experiences can be from twenty years ago or more, or they can be from the present. The important thing is that they made a real difference in your life. Describe each experience in a few words.

- Now review the experiences in your list. Do you see a pattern? Is there a theme or two that connects them? What's the pattern? What are the themes?

  _____

  _____

  _____

- What do the patterns and themes tell you about what creates meaning for you? About your hopes and dreams for the future?

  _____

  _____

  _____

  _____

## REFLECTION 2

Imagine that you are attending a dinner given by your colleagues five years from now, honoring you as "The Leader of the Year." One after the other, your colleagues and family talk about the contributions you have made to them, the organization, and to the community. What do you hope that they will say about you?

_____

_____

_____

_____

- What you want others to say about your contributions is really an expression of your own dreams. What does your description of what you want others to say tell you about the difference you'd like to make in the world?

_____

_____

_____

_____

_____

_____

## APPLICATION 1

## Find Your Theme

Focusing on the project you've chosen, what truly inspires and excites you about it?

_____

_____

_____

_____

_____

_____

_____

_____

_____

_____

- Beyond its business, financial, or organizational objectives, what higher meaning or purpose does (or could) this project serve?

_____

_____

_____

_____

- What future trend(s)—demographics, technology, and so forth—are likely to influence the direction of this project? For example, we know that younger workers, "the Millennials," are different from the Boomers. Both may be a part of your desired future, and data indicates that they have some different, and potentially competing, values. This trend would influence your project in the sense that you will need to find ways to accommodate both sets of values and be prepared to resolve conflicts.

_____

_____

_____

_____

• What future trends are likely to influence what you aspire to achieve?

_____

_____

_____

_____

_____

## APPLICATION 2

## Check the Fit

As you did with your values, you need to do a fitness check with the vision you are beginning to articulate.

- Are you clear about the organization's vision? If not, where do you need clarity, and how are you going to find it?

_____

_____

_____

_____

_____

Now compare your personal aspirations for your project to the organization's vision. If there appears to be alignment between your vision and the organization's vision, move on to the next application exercise. If not, determine how you are going to resolve the conflict.

As you did with Model the Way, you can engage in a dialogue with your manager about the situation. Another way is to talk it over with your family or a close colleague. Sometimes we find that the conflict is a result of a lack of clarity, and other times it's because we can't figure out how to meet our needs and the organization's at the same time. Whatever the root cause, this is something that you need to address. You will not be able to lead others to a place you personally do not want to go.

☐ There is alignment. (Move on.)
☐ There is a conflict. I will do the following to resolve it:

_____

_____

_____

_____

## APPLICATION 3

### Discover Common Ground

Engage your project team in a conversation about the same questions that you answered in Application 1. You can hold that conversation over a series of meetings or on a retreat. You can do it one-on-one or in a group. However you do it, it's important to hear about each person's hopes, dreams, and aspirations. At the conclusion of these conversations, help the group find common themes among the individual aspirations by asking the questions below.

### NOTE

If you have not assembled your team yet, do this activity when you have.

- What are the common themes that weave our dreams and hopes into one tapestry?

_____

_____

_____

_____

- How does this project contribute to the larger vision of the organization?

_____

_____

_____

_____

_____

# APPLICATION 4

## Give Life to the Vision

The practice that most differentiates leaders from other credible people is their ability to Inspire a Shared Vision. You have to be comfortable talking about your unique and ideal image of the future. You need to write and rehearse speaking your "vision statement," whether you deliver it to one person at a time or to one hundred.

You give life to a vision when you infuse it with powerful language, with metaphors, stories, word pictures, and other figures or statements. Think of a vision as a song. If a song were about the theme of "love," it would be pretty hard to sell it if it just repeated that one word over and over again. All songs that stand the test of time are variations on a theme, and the words in those songs have a unique way of expressing that theme. Your vision statement needs to do the same.

The following exercises are intended to help you develop a vision statement that will resonate with your audience—one that will be remembered and repeated.

Before you write your own, here's an example of an inspiring vision statement that a project leader put together:

> We have a very noble and important mission before us—one that will contribute to the liberation of our employees. In talking to all of you about what you believe we are here to accomplish, it's clear that together we share the aspiration of making the work of our colleagues effortless and the experience of our customers joyful.
>
> In so many organizations policies and procedures are like heavy stones around the necks of employees. Even saying the words "policies and procedures" makes people groan. They weigh us down. They get in the way of innovation and growth. They make employees and customers furious. They make me furious! We are embarking on an honorable quest to remove those mighty stones from around our necks and use them instead as building blocks for a future in which we can and we will flourish.
>
> Over the next two years, we will work together to create fully integrated and interactive systems for financial tracking and reporting. From where we are

today, that may seem like trying to build the Pyramids of Giza. It's a huge project, with a lot of pieces that have to come together smoothly, but it is possible.

Policies and procedures, when justly established, equitably administered, and rapidly executed, are essential to every organization's effectiveness and fairness. Without them, life would be arbitrary, uncertain, and subjective. Even dangerous.

The basic policies and procedures we're putting in place today are the building blocks. As we build each system, we'll be putting more stones in place. Then merging and integrating the systems will be the "capstone" that completes this awe-inspiring accomplishment.

Along the way, we may become discouraged—we may find there are too many stones, the stones are too heavy, there aren't enough of us. But I know that the organization is committed to this project and will give us what we need to complete it. The final system will have all the elegance and durability of the pyramids. People will be able to access timely, relevant, reliable, and secure information from their desktops. No more hunting for current numbers, and all the glitches that arise from systems that are not integrated. People will feel like a weight has been lifted and that they can operate more freely and responsibly.

Picture their faces when:
- The sales rep accesses current cost information from her laptop and beats the competitor's proposal by three days and 20 percent.
- The service technician accesses accurate inventory data and can confidently promise delivery dates to a customer.

This is what we can—and will—create together. We will make it possible.

## Envision the Future

Picture yourself, your team, and your organization at the end of this project. It has been successful beyond your wildest dreams. What do you see? Describe it in rich detail by responding to the questions and instructions that follow.

- What are people doing?

_____
_____
_____
_____
_____
_____
_____
_____
_____
_____

- What are people saying?

_____
_____
_____
_____
_____
_____
_____
_____
_____
_____
_____

- How are people feeling?

_____

_____

_____

_____

_____

_____

_____

_____

_____

_____

- What positive things are happening as a result?

_____

_____

_____

_____

_____

_____

_____

_____

_____

_____

_____

## *Use Metaphor*

The most powerful visions use metaphor or visual analogy to change abstract notions into tangible and memorable images. Here's an example:

| *Metaphor* | *How It's Like This Project* |
|---|---|
| Skyscraper | Ambitious, expensive |
| | Reaches upward to the sky |
| | Requires a team and lots of coordination |
| | Requires different kinds of material to make it strong and beautiful |

Take a few minutes to identify a concrete object or activity that could serve as a metaphor for your project, one that might be inspiring if your team and other stakeholders hold it in mind. For example, you could say your project is like:

- A marathon
- The ascent of Mt. Everest
- The America's Cup yacht race
- An eagle's flight
- A revolution
- A tall redwood

Now, try this for yourself. First, take three minutes to brainstorm and record below a list of as many metaphors—figures of speech that suggest a likeness between your project and something else—as you can.

My project is like:

_____

_____

_____

_____

From your list, select the metaphor that works best for you and your project. Explain how your project is like your metaphorical expression.

| *Metaphor* | *How It's Like This Project* |
|---|---|
| _____ | _____ |
| _____ | _____ |
| _____ | _____ |
| _____ | _____ |
| _____ | _____ |

## *Enlist Others*

Now take a few moments to think about the people whom you want your vision to inspire. Who are they? Be sure to include as many groups as you can identify: customers, shareholders, and vendors, as well as team members. What motivates them? Study the example below.

Audience: *Shareholders*
Motivators: *Profit, future growth, competitive advantage*

Audience: _____

Motivators: _____

Audience: _____

Motivators: _____

Audience: _____

Motivators: _____

Audience: _____

Motivators: _____

Now review what you have written with one objective in mind: to identify what these audiences have in common. What can you do to appeal to their overlapping interests? For example, let's say one of the motivators they share is the chance to learn new things. How can you help all of them advance their learning? You might send each to a training program, form a book club, have brown-bag lunches to discuss what's being learned from the project, invite an author of a relevant book to speak to the group, or go on a site visit to another organization that is engaged in a related project but in a different industry.

| *What They Have in Common* | *How I Can Appeal to This Motivator* |
| --- | --- |
| _____ | _____ |
| _____ | _____ |
| _____ | _____ |
| _____ | _____ |
| _____ | _____ |

# APPLICATION 5

## Vision Statement

As a culmination of all the thinking you've done in this section, you are now going to write a compelling vision statement for your project. Do you remember how we defined vision at the beginning of this chapter? If not, take a moment to review. Then answer the questions below to formulate the key components of your vision statement.

• What ideal inspires you—gives you passion—for this project?

_____

_____

_____

_____

_____

_____

_____

• What ideal(s) would inspire the other constituents on this project?

_____

_____

_____

_____

_____

_____

- What is *unique* about the dream you and your constituents have for this project?

  _____

  _____

  _____

  _____

  _____

- What *future* do you envision for your constituents and for the greater organization or community?

  _____

  _____

  _____

  _____

  _____

- How does this vision serve the *common good*: the good of all essential constituents?

  _____

  _____

  _____

  _____

  _____

- What metaphors or visual *image(s)* can you provide that appeal to others?

_____

_____

_____

_____

_____

Now pull all the pieces together and write your vision statement in four to seven paragraphs on the blank lines that follow.

## MY VISION STATEMENT

_____

_____

_____

_____

_____

_____

_____

_____

_____

_____

_____

_____

_____

_____

_____

# APPLICATION 6

## Try It Out

Going live with your vision statement is like taking a theatrical performance to Broadway. The show doesn't open until weeks or months of rehearsals and a tryout off-Broadway or out of town to work out the rough spots. Similarly, you need to rehearse your vision statement, asking colleagues, coaches, and friends who can give you honest feedback to play the role of your "loving critics."

• Who are some trusted friends or colleagues you can approach to "test run" your vision?

_____

_____

_____

_____

_____

• When will you do these rehearsals?

_____

_____

_____

• Who's really good at Inspire a Shared Vision who can act as your coach? (A coach is someone who can help you build your skills, not just give you feedback.)

_____

_____

_____

• Once you feel comfortable with your statement and your presentation, select a time and a place or occasion to "go live"—to "open on Broadway." What is that time and place?

_____

_____

_____

After you have made your vision presentation, how will you know whether or not your audience is genuinely inspired? For example, when people are inspired they smile, applaud, show excitement, and talk a lot about how meaningful and unique the project is. Someone might say, "This is the most exciting project I have worked on in ten years," "I never knew that something that seemed so ordinary could become so truly extraordinary," or "I feel as if I'm growing" and "I'm contributing to something really important."

• Think about the signals other people will be sending that will tell you they are inspired and record them below.

_____

_____

_____

_____

_____

_____

_____

_____

_____

_____

_____

_____

## IMPLICATIONS

What have you learned about yourself as a leader from the activities in this chapter?

_____

_____

_____

_____

_____

_____

Based on your experience with these application exercises, what do you need to do in order to improve how you Inspire a Shared Vision during this project?

_____

_____

_____

_____

_____

_____

**CHAPTER 6**

# CHALLENGE THE PROCESS

**PEOPLE DO THEIR BEST** when there's the chance to transform the way things are. Leaders seek and accept challenging opportunities to test their abilities, and they motivate others as well to exceed their self-perceived limits. They treat every assignment as an adventure, not just another routine.

Most innovations do not come from leaders—they come from the people closest to the work. They also come from what we call "outsight." Exemplary leaders look for good ideas everywhere. They venture out and listen, take advice, and learn.

Exemplary leaders move forward in small steps with little victories. They test and they take risks with bold ideas. And because risk taking involves mistakes and failure, leaders accept and grow from the inevitable disappointments. They treat these as learning opportunities.

To Challenge the Process, you *search for opportunities* by seizing the initiative and by looking outward for innovative ways to improve, and you *experiment and take risks* by constantly generating small wins and learning from experience.

Here are examples from personal-best cases we've collected of how several leaders Challenge the Process:

*To get members of his product development team to question the status quo in the company, a director of development* asks everyone on the team to imagine that they have just left their jobs to join a startup that is intent on putting their former company out of business. He then asks them to generate in thirty minutes as many ways to do this as they can think of. The ensuing discussion is rich with all kinds of new possibilities.

*A new plant manager* was brought in to improve the quality of her plant's production process. In order to communicate that "things are going to be different," she had the floors cleaned, walls painted, and employee washrooms renovated. This grabbed people's attention, demonstrated that quality is in the little details—it's hard to produce quality products in a dirty facility—and made it clear that she was serious about starting quickly.

*To increase the flow of new menu ideas into his restaurant, the chef* treats his servers and cooks to a meal at any restaurant with cuisine similar to theirs. The employees return with written and oral reports on what they learn.

*The new director of science and technology at a university* needed to increase the number of research grants coming into the university. He wanted his faculty to more freely exchange ideas and engage in conversation so that they could come up with some innovative ideas. His first action was to put blackboards on the hall walls in the physics building so that spontaneous scientific discussions could occur anywhere and at any time.

*The leader of a project team in a bank* looking at how to enhance service sent her team members to a department store known for its customer orientation so they could experience service quality there and bring back suggestions on how to apply those ideas at the bank.

*The principal of a suburban school* faced problems that were numerous and deep. He had to, in his words, "breathe new life into an organization that was on hold." He knew he needed to do something radical. He decided that the best way to do that was to create a significantly different scheduling structure that no other school in the district had. He was the first to challenge years and years of the traditional scheduling process.

The new president of a charitable organization wanted to change the culture from one where people were reluctant to take risks for fear of failure to one in which everyone admits and learns from mistakes. So at the end of a fundraising drive he conducted a "postmortem" during which everyone talked about what they learned, what went well, what went poorly, and what they could do better the next time. He was also the first to admit his mistakes so that others felt more comfortable in doing the same.

## OBJECTIVES

As a result of completing the worksheets in this chapter you will be better able to:

- Identify opportunities in your project that would benefit from innovative approaches
- Engage your team members in generating and selecting innovative solutions
- Implement methods for learning from the inevitable mistakes of challenging the status quo
- Identify incremental steps you can take to implement changes and to create a sense of forward momentum

# Reflect & Apply

Answer the following reflection questions.

- What have you changed lately?

_____

_____

_____

_____

_____

- What "daring failure" have you experienced in your life? How did you handle it? What did you learn? Be specific.

_____

_____

_____

_____

_____

_____

- What do you find fun and rewarding about taking risks and trying new things?

_____

_____

_____

_____

_____

- What do you find difficult about taking risks and trying new things?

_____

_____

_____

_____

_____

# APPLICATION 1

## Check for Limiting Assumptions

In every sector, industry, organization, program, and group, it seems that even before you start a project there are things that limit what you can do. You know, the "We can't do that because . . ." responses you often hear when you propose doing something innovative and different. Some of these reasons for not doing something new are real and rational, and some are imagined and emotional.

- What are the "We can't do that because . . ." statements that you've made, you've heard, or you expect to hear that may constrain your project?

  For example:

- We don't use outside contractors to do core parts of our jobs.
- We don't have enough time.
- We have insufficient staffing.
- We have an inadequate budget for temps.
- There are other pressing management priorities.
- There are too many conflicting commitments.
- List the "We can't do it because . . ." statements that may constrain your project:

  _____

  _____

  _____

  _____

  _____

- Ask your team members to make the same list.

- Post the combined list of statements where everyone can see them. Then do the following:

  - Put a plus (+) sign next to those statements that are really true, for example, some law of nature, a governmental law, or an ethical value prevents you from doing something.

  - Put a minus (–) sign next to those statements that are not true or may be true but can be challenged.

  - Put a check (√) next to those limiting assumptions that you want to challenge in the planning and execution of this project. You may not want to challenge all the ones you put a minus (–) sign by, but check as many as you can. Stretch yourself and your team to search for opportunities and experiment, but don't stretch yourselves to the breaking point.

  - Prominently post this list. You and your team will come back to it again as you think of ways to Challenge the Process and more "We can't do that because . . ." assumptions appear.

## APPLICATION 2

### Look Outside

The best leaders and the most successful organizations do not assume that they have all the ideas they need. They know that the source of creative and innovative ideas on how to do things differently is more likely to be outside their boundaries. They are net importers of ideas. For example, to exercise "outsight" you might:

- Arrange a field trip that would stimulate your group's thinking.
- Read magazines from fields you know nothing about.
- Call three customers or clients and ask them what they would like to see your group do that you are not now doing.
- Go shopping at a competitor's store or website.
- Bring a client or customer into one of your project planning meetings and ask the person to share his or her ideas.
- How can you search outside of your project and your organization to discover unexpected ideas? Now make your own list:

_____

_____

_____

_____

_____

## APPLICATION 3

### Innovate and Create

Gather your team together to complete this activity. Explain that behind every apparent limitation is an opportunity waiting to be discovered. Say that you are going to ask them to think outside the box—literally! By doing so, they can transform how they approach any obstacle.

Share this example of thinking (and writing) outside the box:

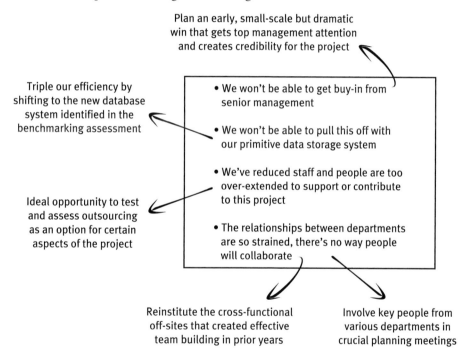

As a group, refer back to your team's list of limiting assumptions. To Challenge the Process, identify a way to turn each limitation that you checked above into an opportunity to grow. Review the potential sources of frustration and limitations you listed earlier. Look at the ones you checked—the ones you want to challenge.

Draw a box on a flip chart, whiteboard, or online collaboration tool for all team members to see. Write the limitations you want to challenge in the box. Draw arrows from each limitation to a point outside the box, as in the previous example, and write an opportunity for each limitation.

## APPLICATION 4

### Check the Fit

Before you embark on making any changes, make sure you and your project team members talk about how this all fits with the vision and values. Take a few minutes to discuss and record how all the innovative things you want to do contribute to the realization of the vision and can be guided by the shared values.

_____

_____

_____

_____

_____

_____

## APPLICATION 5

### Take the Initiative

As we said in discussing Model the Way, leaders go first. If you want others to be proactive in searching for opportunities and taking risks, then you need to be the first to demonstrate those behaviors. Focus on yourself, and record how you will take the initiative.

*   The status quo I'll challenge and overturn:

_____

_____

_____

_____

_____

_____

*   The experiments I'll try:

_____

_____

_____

_____

_____

_____

- The places where I'll look for new ideas:

  _____

  _____

  _____

  _____

  _____

- The ways in which I'll reward failure (For example: You could give the Stuffed Giraffe Award when people stick their necks out, or the Edison Award for failing lots of times on the way to inventing something new and different. You could give a few lottery tickets to someone who "took a chance." Be creative, and send the message that you want people to take risks and learn.)

  _____

  _____

  _____

  _____

  _____

- The immovable obstacles I'll demolish:

  _____

  _____

  _____

  _____

  _____

- Other ways I'll take the initiative to change, grow, and make improvements:

_____

_____

_____

_____

_____

# APPLICATION 6

## Encourage Initiative in Others

Remember, you can't do it alone! You need to model Challenge the Process, and you need to create a climate in which others can do the same.

Ask your team members to answer the questions you answered in Application 5. List those questions on a sheet of paper or your collaboration tool and give your team members time to respond. It should only take them about thirty minutes. They can do it as pre-work for a team meeting or they can do it in a meeting. The important thing is that everyone participates in the process.

After people have written down their ideas, and before they share them with each other, ask them to respond to the following:

- In order for me to feel safe in taking this risk, I need you (the leader of this team) to. . . .

Record the responses so everyone can see them. Make a copy for yourself. Give team members one of the following responses to each request:

- "Yes, I will do that. No problem."
- "I can do that, AND in order for me to do it, here's what I need."
- "No, I won't do that, because. . . ." For each thing you will not do, the team deserves to know a reason why. It's a sign of respect to explain your response.

# IMPLICATIONS

What have you learned about yourself as a leader from the activities in this chapter?

_____

_____

_____

_____

_____

_____

Based on your experience with these application exercises, what do you need to do in order to improve how you Challenge the Process during this project?

_____

_____

_____

_____

_____

_____

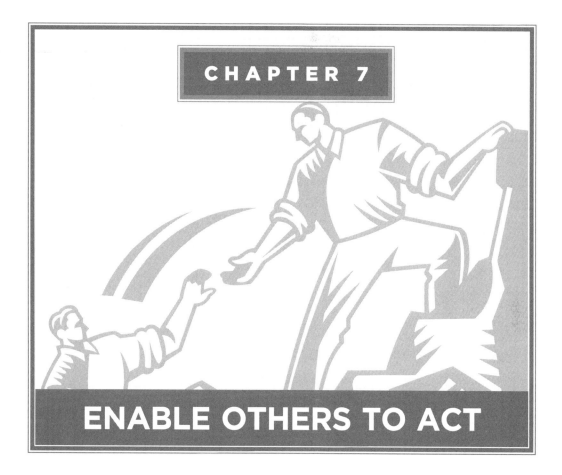

CHAPTER 7

ENABLE OTHERS TO ACT

**LEADERS KNOW THAT** they can't make extraordinary things happen all by themselves. It takes partners, so leaders invest in building spirited and cohesive teams, teams that feel like family. They develop collaborative goals and cooperative relationships with colleagues. They know that these relationships are the keys that unlock support.

Mutual respect is what sustains extraordinary group efforts. Leaders build the skills and abilities of their constituents to deliver on commitments. They create a climate where people feel in control of their own lives.

To Enable Others to Act, you *foster collaboration* by building trust and facilitating relationships, and you *strengthen others* by increasing self-determination and developing competence.

Here are examples from personal-best cases we've collected of how leaders Enable Others to Act:

*A vice president of property services* is given the assignment to double available workstations at an already crowded facility—in nine months. In a series of meetings with her team, she asks them to evaluate alternatives and set a plan of action. Once the team does so, she entrusts them with implementing it. Her role is to make sure people are organized, on schedule, and headed in the same direction. She also intervenes if teamwork breaks down or problems fall between the cracks. She provides lots of feedback throughout the process.

*A school principal at an underperforming school* needs to make some radical changes in order to improve student achievement. As part of this major project, he creates an Instructional Leadership Team made up of respected teacher-leaders and gives them the discretion to determine curriculum. To show support for this team, at curriculum meetings only teachers sit at the discussion table. Administrators sit in chairs around the team to signal they are there to support, and not decide.

*The chief information officer of a global technical, professional, and construction services company* was charged with rolling out a worldwide safety and leadership program to the IT organization. Rather than leading the discussions herself, or having someone in the training department do it, she asked everyone in the first two layers of the IT organization to lead at least one workshop, and to try to make each workshop a mixture of attendees from multiple IT groups. In three months they involved over eight hundred members of global IT in more than twenty-five different sessions of the workshop. Everyone who led it agreed that he or she got as much out of facilitating the workshop as any of the participants and that the experience remained fresh even facilitating multiple times.

*When the incoming commander of a U.S. Navy ship* took over, morale was terrible and performance was the worst in the service. He knew he had to do something immediately to turn the situation around. He decided that he would spend one hour with each of the 310 sailors just talking about them and their needs. In the process of listening and paying attention, he not only built rapport and understanding, but he also gathered ideas about how to improve the ship that when implemented saved the Navy millions of dollars.

*A manufacturing executive* facing a possible plant closure trained all employees to read and interpret financial statements. The company's financial information is shared and discussed regularly—by machine workers and clerical staff as well as management. The company not only has avoided bankruptcy but has become consistently profitable by expecting everyone in the company to act as a business owner.

*An American financial services executive* was appointed the managing director of one of its foreign offices. Because he was an outsider, he was viewed with skepticism. Rather than jump in with all kinds of changes, his first acts were just to get to know people—who they were, what motivated them, what things they liked to do, and what they thought they could do collectively to achieve things. These early acts of relying on "local experts" quickly earned him respect and enabled all of them to significantly improve services.

## OBJECTIVES

As a result of completing the worksheets in this chapter, you'll be better able to:

- Build supportive relationships with your project team members
- Develop the competence and confidence of team members
- Develop cooperative working relationships among team members
- Connect team members to the people they need to get extraordinary things done

# Reflect & Apply

Think of a time when, as a direct result of something a leader said or did, you felt personally powerful and capable. Write down the actions the leader took that contributed to your feeling powerful, strong, capable, and effective—the master of your own experience. Be as specific as you can.

_____

_____

_____

_____

_____

Now think of a time when you felt powerless, weak, and insignificant as a result of something a leader said or did. What specifically did he or she do?

_____

_____

_____

_____

_____

Recall a time when you were part of a team that "just clicked"—a time when it seemed as if everyone was working together smoothly and effortlessly. Describe how people acted toward one another and what the team leader did that contributed to making the team work.

_____

_____

_____

_____

_____

_____

Using the lessons from your own experiences—as an individual and as a team member—ask yourself, "How can I enable others to feel powerful and avoid diminishing their personal effectiveness? How can I contribute to teamwork and trust?" Record your responses.

_____

_____

_____

_____

_____

_____

_____

_____

_____

Ask yourself, "In what ways will making others feel powerful and creating a climate of teamwork and trust benefit this project?" Record your responses.

_____

_____

_____

_____

_____

_____

_____

_____

_____

_____

_____

# APPLICATION 1

## Ask Questions, Listen, and Take Advice

Leadership is a relationship, and a healthy relationship is based on trust. Trust is fostered by listening and attending to the other person.

If you have not already done so, schedule a sixty-minute one-on-one relationship-building meeting with each of your project team members. During these meetings, ask a lot of questions, and then listen carefully. When you do share information, be as self-disclosing and open as you can be. Here are the kinds of questions you should ask during the one-on-one meetings:

- What do you want to get out of your experience as a member of this project team?
- What motivates you to do the best work you can?
- What can I do to support you in getting what you want out of this experience?
- How would you characterize the relationships among the team members right now? (You might need to skip or delay this question if the team has just been formed.)
- What can I do to help create and maintain a climate of teamwork and trust?
- What talents and skills do you bring to this project?
- What can I do to help you sharpen your talents and strengthen your skills?
- What do you like most about being part of this project?
- What do you like least about being part of this project?
- What would have to happen during the project for you to be able to look back later and say, "This was the best project I was ever a part of"? What actions would you have to see and/or what events would you have to experience for you honestly to say, "This was the best"?
- What specific recommendations do you have about how we can improve the way we do our work on this project? (You may want to skip or delay this question if your team has just been formed.)

## APPLICATION 2

### Ensure Self-Leadership

After you have completed your interviews, complete a Power Profile for each person on your project team. Write down what each person needs so he or she can lead or be self-led. (You have our permission to reproduce the Power Profile on pages 99 and 100 for each team member.)

# POWER PROFILE

Team Member: _____

 Project Role: _____

 What unique perspective does this person bring to our team?

_____

_____

_____

_____

 Which of this person's strengths and skills will be most useful to our team?

_____

_____

_____

_____

 What kind of training and support might help this person become a stronger team member?

_____

_____

_____

_____

What opportunities can I provide for this person to assume greater responsibility or achieve greater visibility?

_____

_____

_____

_____

What information does this person require to work productively?

_____

_____

_____

_____

What opportunities can I provide for this person to work collaboratively with other team members?

_____

_____

_____

_____

What are areas in which this person could be more effective, and how can I help him or her improve?

_____

_____

_____

_____

# APPLICATION 3

## Develop Competence and Confidence

Review your team members' Power Profiles. For each person on the team, identify at least one action that you can take to increase his or her confidence and personal capacity to perform.

*Examples*

Team Member: *Janaid*

One Action to Enable This Team Member to Act: *Feels powerful when he has the right information. Put him in touch with Betty in Information Technology for systems assistance.*

Team Member: *Sharon*

One Action to Enable This Team Member to Act: *Feels powerful when she has strong skills. Says she needs training in time management. Send her to a course on time management and then provide the tools to help her use those skills daily.*

Team Member: *Jose Luis*

One Action to Enable This Team Member to Act: *Highly experienced in his field, and feels powerful when he has the personal discretion to make decisions. Make sure to use a contracting process in which, from the beginning, we agree on what's expected, and then "get out of his way." Set up regular sessions in which I consult with him on progress.*

Team Member: _____

One Action to Enable This Team Member to Act

_____

_____

_____


Team Member: _____

One Action to Enable This Team Member to Act

_____

_____

_____


Team Member: _____

One Action to Enable This Team Member to Act

_____

_____

_____


Team Member: _____

One Action to Enable This Team Member to Act

_____

_____

_____


If you have more than four team members, photocopy this page or continue on another sheet of paper.

## APPLICATION 3

## Develop Cooperative Goals

Based on your interviews, there are likely to be things that all or most of your team members want from the project and want to accomplish through the project. What are the goals that people share in common? What motivations are shared?

_____

_____

_____

_____

_____

What actions can you take to build on these shared motivations and goals to create a sense that "We're all in this together"?

For example:

- Let's say one of the shared motivations is to learn from others. To do that you hold weekly team meetings where everyone reports on something new he or she learned that week—a new method of doing the work, the name of a contact who is a great resource, or an effective way to reduce stress.

- Let's say a common goal is have the project recognized for its contribution to the advancement of the field. You could assign someone to document what is done and someone to write a journal article, and then make sure that the team submits a proposal to present a paper at a professional conference.

- Let's say that a shared motivation is to have fun. You could hold weekly celebrations at which everyone is encouraged to "brag" about something neat he or she did that week; pass out inexpensive toys to liven up meetings; or encourage a musician on your team to entertain during a break.

Actions you can take to build on shared goals and motivations:

_____

_____

_____

_____

_____

_____

_____

# APPLICATION 3

## Make Connections

It's not just what you know and what you can do that gets things done. It's also who you know. If your team members are going to perform at their best, they need to be directly connected to the right people for important sources of support—information, materials, money, and so on.

In the old world of work, the manager controlled access to these sources, but in today's world of online intelligence and flatter organizations, that old approach only slows things down. You need to set up the connections and then let your team members deal directly with their sources of power.

One tool for helping you to map out who needs to be connected to whom is a *sociogram*. A sociogram is simply a graphic representation of the relationships in a group. There's an example on the next page.

To create a sociogram for people on your project:

- Draw a circle in the middle of a blank sheet of paper or your collaboration tool. Put the name of a team member in the circle.
- Surrounding this name, draw circles representing the critical people to whom this person needs to be connected in order to do his or her best. There may be half a dozen or more critical people.
- Below each person's name, indicate the kind of "resource" needed. For instance, the resource could be information, money, the ability to teach a critical skill, approval, access to other people, and so forth.
- Draw lines to connect the people who should know each other or should be directly connected with each other in some way. If two people should be closely connected—that is, they should interact frequently—draw a thick line to connect them. If two people should interact somewhat often, draw a thin line to connect them. If two people should know each other, but they have no need to interact directly, then draw a dotted line.
- Step back and see what this visual tells you about what needs to be done in this situation.

Look at the example. Let's imagine that Jim is on your team, and he's writing a technical manual that is on the critical path of the project. Around Jim are the individuals who are most critical to his success.

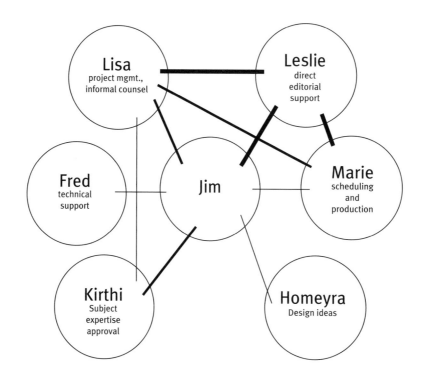

What does this sociogram tell you? It's clear that Leslie and Lisa are the most critical people to Jim in this project. Kirthi also plays an important role. If Jim is going to do the best he can, he has to be empowered to work closely with these individuals. The sociogram also shows that there are critical connections that need to exist between Leslie and Lisa and Leslie, Lisa, and Marie, and Leslie and Marie. If you were the project leader in this situation, you would want to pay attention to these relationships even if you did not have direct control over them.

Now use another blank paper to draw a sociogram for yourself.

When you have finished your own sociogram, meet with all members of your immediate team to create their individual sociograms.

**107**

ENABLE OTHERS TO ACT

Review your team members' sociograms. What do you need to do to make sure that each one of them is connected to critical sources of power so they have the "energy" to do their best?

_____

_____

_____

_____

_____

_____

_____

_____

_____

_____

_____

_____

_____

_____

_____

_____

_____

_____

_____

_____

_____

_____

# IMPLICATIONS

What have you learned about yourself as a leader from the activities in this chapter?

_____

_____

_____

_____

_____

_____

_____

_____

Based on your experience with these application exercises, what do you need to do in order to improve how you Enable Others to Act during this project?

_____

_____

_____

_____

_____

_____

_____

_____

_____

_____

_____

_____

_____

**CHAPTER 8**

# ENCOURAGE THE HEART

**MAKING EXTRAORDINARY THINGS HAPPEN IN ORGANIZATIONS** is hard work. Leaders encourage their followers' hearts to go the distance. They visibly acknowledge people's efforts in pursuit of the common vision. With a thank-you note, a smile, and public praise, they let others know how much they mean to the organization.

Leaders also express pride in the accomplishments of their teams. They make a point of telling the rest of the organization about what the teams have achieved. Celebration is important to a winning team. Leaders find ways to mark accomplishments. They take time out to rejoice in reaching a milestone and to gather spirit and support to continue.

To Encourage the Heart, you *recognize contributions* by showing appreciation for individual excellence, and you *celebrate the values and victories* by creating a spirit of community.

Here are examples from the personal-best cases we've collected of how leaders Encourage the Heart:

*The new coach of a high school football team* took the same team of boys who'd had a losing season the prior year and applied a positive approach to creating a winning season the next year. His method was simple. Instead of always pointing out the negatives, he would always start with "Here's what you guys did right," and then "Here are two or three things you can improve on." He also required the team members to stay positive with each other.

*The senior vice president of learning and education in one financial services company* wanted to encourage her training group to take greater risks. She helped the process along by creating the Giraffe Award, given, naturally enough, for sticking your neck out. Recipients were recognized in front of the group each month with a stuffed giraffe and a colored poster, and the stories of their contributions were told to all. Each time, the award was given by the prior recipient and it was personalized with something particularly unique to the new honoree.

*The senior vice president of a bank* wanted to do something special for one employee who had reached a personal milestone. To make the public recognition special, he staged a "This Is Your Life" production, complete with a conference call with the employee's mother.

*The general manager and executive chef of a university faculty club* sent an "Open Letter of Thanks" to club members, university departments, and club staff in which she described in glowing detail the celebration of the club's dramatic turnaround at the end of a year-long effort.

*When his team reaches a key milestone, a project manager* makes the rounds to shake the hand of each team member, takes several key team members to lunch, calls each team member with a personal thanks for his or her effort and contributions, and hosts a small cake-and-coffee celebration party.

*A plant manager* creates monthly "super person" award ceremonies in which she recognizes people who make special contributions to improving productivity or reducing costs. At each ceremony, she presents a creatively chosen, humorous gift that symbolizes what the person has done and tells the story of why that person is receiving the award.

*During the Christmas rush at one retail store, the owner* wanted to create a sense of community that would engage the temporary staff hired for the season. He installed a "Bragging Board" at the employee entrance, and whenever he wanted to acknowledge an employee for an achievement, he wrote a quick thank-you note and posted it on the Bragging Board. Soon employees started attaching their own notes of thanks and celebration.

*The director of operations* took on the project of turning around the sales of his company. To capture everyone's attention, he used what he called the "closing coat." Whenever a sale was made, the sales force would select someone to wear the "closing coat"—a bright yellow polyester jacket. The coat-wearer would then walk around the company with the director of operations and tell the story of the sale. When people saw someone wearing the coat they knew they were one step closer to their goal.

## OBJECTIVES

As a result of completing the worksheets in this chapter, you will be better able to:

* Recognize individuals for their contributions to the success of the project
* Tell recognition stories that will recognize individuals and reinforce key values and standards
* Celebrate team accomplishments
* Build informal social support among team members

# Reflect & Apply

Think back over the times when someone has personally recognized and rewarded you for outstanding performance—the times when someone showed genuine appreciation for what you accomplished.

Select one time that you would consider your most memorable recognition—a time when you felt the most appreciated by someone. Recall the story in as much vivid detail as you can.

- What made this time so memorable? Why did you select this particular experience?

_____

_____

_____

- Make a special note of what the other person did to recognize you. What actions did he or she take? What did he or she do? Describe the setting, the other person's actions, and your feelings.

_____

_____

_____

_____

_____

_____

_____

_____

# APPLICATION 1

## Recognize Individual Contributions

Recognizing individual contributions to the values and the achievements of your project is your opportunity not only to Encourage the Heart of your team members but also to reinforce your project values.

In the chapter on Model the Way, your team agreed on shared values. Recognition for individual contributions to the project should always be framed in the context of those values.

- Refer back to your list of values. Note what each desired value looks like in terms of on-the-job behavior. The best way to generate more of the behavior you want is to watch for examples of people who are doing things right. Don't wait for a special occasion to say thank you; recognize them as soon as possible.

- When you recognize a team member, link the person's action to the value he or she exemplified. This serves to reinforce the value, and it also provides an illustration of what others can do to contribute. For example, you might say something like "The other day, I saw our project veteran, Kellie, coaching one of our newest team members on how to use our sales tracking software. She took time away from her own calls to help someone else. I'll never forget what she said: 'I know you can do it! You're very talented.' Wow! Kellie demonstrated to the rest of us our value of teamwork. Kellie, come on up here. I know you love hockey, so the special 'Stanley Cup' [a tiny replica of the trophy] goes to you, along with these two tickets to the next home game of our local hockey team. Thanks, Kellie."

- Check in: Do you honestly believe that every member of your team is capable of acting, and will act, to achieve the goals you have set and live by the values you have agreed on? If you do, make sure you express it in words and deeds. If you do not, you'll find that you are going to have a tough time being very authentic and genuine in recognizing contributions.

- For you to help others do their best, you need to believe in their capacity to perform. If you find yourself doubting the abilities of anyone on your team, it's time for you to take action. Sit down with that person and learn as much as you can about his or her skills and abilities, interests, and particular strengths; where the person thinks he or she needs new skills; and whether he or she thinks this project is a good fit. Find a strength on which you can focus. Find the best fit for the person in the project. Send people, when feasible, to a class to improve their skills. Do something to increase your own confidence in all your team members.

- Personalize your recognition of an individual's contributions. Of course, you can only personalize recognition if you know what the person likes and would consider "special." If you can't answer this question for some of your team members, you need to spend more time getting to know them. Here's a hint: Visit their cubicles, offices, or workstations. Check out the pictures on their desks or tables and the curios they keep in their workspace. Listen to things they talk about doing for fun. Ask their co-workers. It's all about paying attention to the person.

As your project progresses, use the Kudos for a Colleague worksheet on the next page to think through how to recognize individuals who make a special contribution to the project by exemplifying one of the project values. Use this as a template each time you prepare for a recognition.

Completing this worksheet regularly is important. Research indicates that people tend to be more engaged in their work when they are recognized at least once each week. That means that if you have ten people on your team, you should do ten Kudos for a Colleague each week. That may seem like a lot, but once you get the hang of it, it should only take about three minutes per person, or thirty minutes out of your schedule. Don't you think it's worth it to spend thirty minutes a week getting higher levels of performance?

*A note of caution:* The purpose of these worksheets is to help you pay attention and make note of what people do that deserves recognition. It is not about filling in the blanks. In the end, the point is to recognize others for their contributions to the success of the project. Use the worksheets as an aid toward that end.

# KUDOS FOR A COLLEAGUE

Team Member: _____

    The shared value that was exemplified: _____

_____

_____

    What did the team member do to exemplify the value? Be very specific and descriptive.

_____

_____

_____

_____

_____

_____

    How can I personalize the recognition? What can I do to make the recognition special for this person?

_____

_____

_____

_____

_____

_____

Where and when will I recognize the person?

_____

_____

_____

_____

Who else should know about this person's achievement and the action this person took to accomplish what she or he did? How can I publicize it?

_____

_____

_____

_____

# APPLICATION 2

## Tell the Story

We all have the potential to make a positive, lasting impression on others through the recognition we give and the appreciation we show. Just look back at your own most memorable recognition—the one you made a note about at the beginning of this chapter. Someone made a lasting and positive impression on you. You, too, can leave such a lasting, positive impression on another person that years from now he or she will tell others that this most memorable recognition came from you. These lasting impressions end up as the stories we tell others, and those stories get passed along, not only as tales of celebration, but also as illustrations of what's important to us and to others.

We want to develop your capacity to Encourage the Heart through the medium of the story so that you can recognize not just one individual, but also so that you can pass along the lessons to everyone else on your team. Stories put a human face on success. They tell us that someone just like us can make it happen. They create organizational role models that everyone can relate to. They put behavior in a real context. Stories make standards—the goals of the project and the values that guide the team—come alive. They move us. They touch us. By telling a story in detail, leaders illustrate what everyone needs to do to live by the values and move toward the goals. They communicate the specific and proper actions that need to be taken to resolve tough choices. They bring people together "around the campfire" to learn and to have fun.

## *Write Your Story*

Recall a time recently when you observed one or more members of your project team contributing to the project's values and goals. Follow the steps below to write the story.

1. *Identify the Actors.* Name the person—or the people—you want to recognize.

_____

_____

_____

2. *Paint the Scene.* Where and when did this happen? Talk about the circumstances. Set the stage and paint the scene. What was the person (or persons) trying to achieve? What was the motivation? (To answer this question, you'll have to know something about this person. This goes back to the need for leaders to pay attention to what's happening in their organizations. To tell a good story you have to pay attention.)

_____

_____

_____

_____

_____

_____

3. *Describe the Actions.* Relate in as much detail as you can what happened. What specifically did this person and/or each of the people involved do?

_____

_____

_____

_____

_____

_____

4. *Tell How It Ended.* Never leave your audience hanging. Tell the listeners what happened in the end. What happened as a result of the actions?

_____

_____

_____

_____

_____

5. *Include a Surprise.* Every great story includes some kind of surprise. Try to add an element of amazement. What makes this story particularly interesting, unique, memorable, funny, or surprising?

_____

_____

_____

_____

6. *Connect to Shared Values.* Every great story has a "moral" at the end—a values-based lesson about what people can learn from the example. What is the shared value (or values) exemplified by what was done?

_____

_____

_____

_____

*Tell Your Story*

Now have fun telling the story. At a regular meeting or at a special event, share this story with your team. A good story will only take three to five minutes to tell, and you can always find that much time at any gathering. Length is not important. What's important is that you authentically communicate how someone genuinely contributed to making the standards of the project come alive.

After you tell your story, take a few minutes alone to reflect on these questions:

• What was the reaction? How did people respond emotionally?

_____

_____

_____

• How did you feel when telling this story? How comfortable were you? To what extent did you feel that your effort was forced?

_____

_____

_____

• Based on the reactions of others, how well did you clearly connect the actions of the central character in your story to the values and standards you were trying to reinforce?

_____

_____

_____

- What did you learn about your ability to tell stories? What can you do to improve your storytelling abilities? For example, you could:
  - Attend the reading of a novel at your local library or bookstore. Pay particular attention to how the author constructs and tells the story. During question and answer, ask how the author got the idea for the story.
  - Keep a journal of things that happen on the project that will make great stories.
  - Listen to a recording of one of your favorite children's stories. Pay attention to how a professional tells a story. (We know that you're probably not working with children. This is about learning to tell stories, and children love stories.)
  - Take a class in storytelling.
  - At dinner with your family, don't just talk about your day, tell a story about it. Describe the rich details of place, people, and feelings. Let your home be your practice stage.

_____

_____

_____

_____

_____

_____

_____

_____

_____

_____

_____

_____

_____

## APPLICATION 3

### Celebrate Team Accomplishments

Every project milestone is an opportunity for team members to celebrate what they have accomplished and gather spirit and momentum to continue. Here's an example:

Project Milestone: *Marketing plan completed*

Team Celebration:

- *End the day early, and have everyone on the team and their families adjourn to a local park where you can all hang out, play volleyball, meet family members, and relax.*
- *Invite a local comedian over to the office for a special show. Provide the performer some "inside jokes" to include in the material.*

For each of your project milestones, brainstorm several fun and meaningful ways for people to celebrate as a team.

Project Milestone: _____

_____

_____

Team Celebration: _____

_____

_____

Project Milestone: _____

_____

_____

Team Celebration: _____

_____

_____

Project Milestone: _____

_____

_____

Team Celebration: _____

_____

_____

Project Milestone: _____

_____

_____

Team Celebration: _____

_____

_____

## APPLICATION 4

# Build Social Support

Public ceremonies serve another powerful purpose. They bring people closer together. In a more virtual world where more and more communication is via new information technologies, it's becoming increasingly difficult for people to find opportunities to be together. We're social animals, and we need each other.

Those who are fortunate enough to have lots of social support are healthier human beings. Social support is absolutely essential to our well-being and our productivity. Celebrating together is one way we can get that essential support.

Think of some ways you can encourage informal social interaction. For example:

- Put a few comfortable chairs at places where people would naturally congregate—for coffee or meals, for sharing office equipment, or other places.
- Put up a "Bragging Board" in a central spot in the office or on your online collaboration tool. Post a couple of thank-you notes, and then encourage others to do the same when they want to make a public recognition.
- At the start of every scheduled meeting, begin by asking people to share something about themselves—their favorite color, favorite sport, a book they read and would recommend, a movie they like, the names of their pets, and other items. Get the group used to revealing information about themselves.
- Stand at the entryway to your team's work area one morning and greet everyone as he or she arrives.

What other ideas can you think of to promote informal interaction?

_____

_____

_____

_____

_____

# IMPLICATIONS

What have you learned about yourself as a leader from the activities in this chapter?

_____

_____

_____

_____

_____

_____

Based on your experience with these application exercise, what do you need to do in order to improve how you Encourage the Heart during this project?

_____

_____

_____

_____

_____

_____

CHAPTER 9

# REFLECTING ON YOUR PERSONAL-BEST LEADERSHIP PROJECT

**THROUGHOUT** *The Leadership Challenge Workbook,* you have been applying The Five Practices of Exemplary Leadership® to a real project in order to make it another one of your Personal-Best Leadership Experiences. Now that the project has been completed—or several significant milestones have been achieved—we encourage you to spend some time reflecting on your experience. Remember, the best leaders are the best learners. To grow as a leader, you need to learn from your experiences so that you are ready to apply those lessons to your next project.

The questions in this chapter take you through the debriefing process for your own project. You can answer these questions on your own, you can gather your team together and answer them as a group, or do both.

When you have finished debriefing, ask yourself, "What do my answers reveal about my leadership practices, about leading, and about how I can be more effective as a leader in the future?" Armed with this new awareness, you'll be ready to tackle your next Personal-Best Leadership Experience with better understanding of and appreciation for what actions and behaviors make a difference.

You may be finished—or nearly finished—with the execution of your Personal-Best Leadership Project, but this debriefing carries an even larger consequence: It's a critical step in the continuing process of your leadership development. Take the time to do it now, and reap the rewards for the rest of your leadership career.

## MY PERSONAL-BEST LEADERSHIP PROJECT

Review what you wrote on the My Personal-Best Leadership Project worksheet in Chapter 3. Then answer these questions:

*   How did you assess your progress during the project? What criteria did you use?

_____

_____

_____

_____

*   Who else besides you evaluated your success? How did he or she measure it?

_____

_____

_____

*   How well did you meet the project goals?

_____

_____

*   How well did your project meet your expected time frame? The budget?

_____

_____

- Which aspects of your project proved to be the most frustrating or difficult? Why?

_____

_____

_____

_____

- What surprised you along the way? Why?

_____

_____

_____

_____

- Write down several adjectives that describe how you now feel about the project (e.g., proud, exhausted, fulfilled, excited . . .).

_____    _____    _____

_____    _____    _____

- How do your current feelings compare to how you felt at the beginning of the project? What's changed? What's the reason for any change?

_____

_____

_____

- Overall, what have you learned about leadership that is a new insight? What have you learned about yourself and your leadership competencies?

_____

_____

_____

_____

## Model the Way

Review all the worksheets you completed in Chapter 4 on Model the Way and answer these questions:

- Which shared values were most important to you in guiding you along the project journey?

_____

_____

_____

_____

- How easy or difficult was it to forge consensus on values? Why do you think this was the case?

_____

_____

_____

_____

- What values were the most important to you and your team in achieving your shared values? How did you model these values?

_____

_____

_____

_____

_____

- What leadership actions proved to be the most significant in creating alignment between the stated values and the values in action? What was most important in creating consistency between values and actions? What remains to be done?

_____

_____

_____

_____

_____

- What did you learn about Model the Way that you can apply to your next project?

_____

_____

_____

_____

_____

## Inspire a Shared Vision

Review what you wrote in all your worksheets in Chapter 5 on Inspire a Shared Vision, and answer these questions:

- What higher purpose has this project served?

_____

_____

_____

- Now that you've completed your project, how does the reality of what you have accomplished compare to what you envisioned? How does it differ? How do you account for the difference?

_____

_____

_____

_____

_____

- What metaphor would you use to describe this project now?

_____

_____

- What did you learn about Inspire a Shared Vision in your organization? What would you do differently the next time?

_____

_____

_____

_____

_____

## Challenge the Process

Review what you wrote in all of your worksheets in Chapter 6 on Challenge the Process, and answer these questions:

- What innovative methods and techniques did you try in this project, and how did they work out? What did you do differently in this project than what you have done in the past that made it one of your best?

_____

_____

_____

_____

_____

- What experiments did you undertake? How successful were they in terms of learning?

_____

_____

_____

_____

- What have you learned about being more comfortable with and willing to think outside the box?

_____

_____

_____

_____

_____

- How did you promote learning from failure and mistakes?

_____

_____

_____

_____

_____

- How did breaking down your project into small wins—incremental "one-hop-at-a-time" actions—help you achieve your goals?

_____

_____

_____

_____

_____

_____

- What have you learned about Challenge the Process in your organization? What would you do differently the next time?

_____

_____

_____

_____

## Enable Others to Act

Review what you wrote on all the worksheets in Chapter 7 on Enable Others to Act, and answer these questions:

- Which enabling actions were the most successful? Why?

_____

_____

_____

_____

- Were the people on your team able to obtain the information they needed? What systems did you establish that facilitated this process?

_____

_____

_____

_____

- Write down some specific examples of when you gave power away. What effect did this have on your constituents? On you?

_____

_____

_____

_____

_____

- What did you do to make your constituents feel powerful? Was this task easier or more difficult than you expected? Why?

_____

_____

_____

_____

_____

- What have you learned about Enable Others to Act in your organization? What would you do differently next time?

_____

_____

_____

_____

_____

# Encourage the Heart

Review what you wrote on all the worksheets in Chapter 8 on Encourage the Heart, and answer these questions:

• What form or forms of recognition had the most positive influence? Why?

_____

_____

_____

• What effect did recognition and celebration have on your team?

_____

_____

_____

• What creative means did you use to recognize individuals?

_____

_____

_____

• What was your most successful team celebration? Why was it effective?

_____

_____

_____

_____

- What have you learned about Encourage the Heart in your organization? What would you do differently the next time?

_____

_____

_____

_____

_____

# TYING IT ALL TOGETHER

Finally, it's time for some broader reflections on what you learned while using *The Leadership Challenge Workbook* to complete your Personal-Best Leadership Project.

- Of all the leadership actions that you took, which three to five do you believe had the most impact on the success of the project?

_____

_____

_____

_____

- What would you do differently for the next project?

_____

_____

_____

_____

- What would you make certain that you continue to do on your next project?

_____

_____

_____

_____

- What are the five most important things you learned about yourself as a leader?

_____

_____

_____

_____

- What are the five most important things you learned about the members of your team?

_____

_____

_____

_____

_____

- Which practice was the easiest to implement? The most difficult? Why?

_____

_____

_____

_____

_____

_____

- What do you feel are your strengths as a leader?

_____

_____

_____

- Where do you need to improve your leadership skills?

_____

_____

_____

- In addition to asking others to complete this workbook for themselves, how can you pass your leadership lessons on—especially to those you might now be coaching or who might be the most likely candidates for assuming leadership roles in the near future?

_____

_____

_____

_____

# CHAPTER 10

## THE CHALLENGE CONTINUES

**IN THIS WORKBOOK**, and in all of our discussions of leadership, we often use the metaphor of a journey to communicate the active, adventurous spirit of leadership. We talk about leaders as pioneers and trailblazers who take people on expeditions to places they've never been. We talk about summits, and milestones, and signposts.

As with most journeys, the leader's journey does not end with a single project. The journey continues with the next project you take on, and the one after that. As the ancient Chinese proverb says, "There is always a higher mountain." You know there will be more challenges along the path of your development as a leader. There will be more opportunities for you to do your personal best.

We hope that you will refer back to the questions we've asked you in this workbook. We hope you will use them the next time you face a challenge, or discover an amazing opportunity, and begin to explore the possibilities of what you and others can do together. We hope you will teach others to ask these questions. And we hope that you will apply this process not only in your job, but also in your community, in your place of worship, and even in your home.

Challenge is the crucible for greatness. Given the daunting challenges we face today, the potential for greatness is phenomenal. There are no shortages of leadership opportunities. Your leadership talents are needed more than ever.

We wish you continuing joy and success on your next leadership challenge.

# Acknowledgments

**IN THE INTRODUCTION TO THIS WORKBOOK,** we quoted Don Bennett, the first amputee to climb Mt. Rainier, in response to our question, "How did you make it to the top?" As we conclude this workbook, another of Don's comments comes to mind. We asked him, "What was the most important lesson you learned?" He replied, "You can't do it alone."

Sometimes writing a book seems like climbing a mountain, and it really is true that without the team of people climbing alongside us or helping out at base camp we'd never have made it. In fact, this project began as a result of questions from the readers of our books and from participants in The Leadership Challenge® Workshop. They are always eager for practical knowledge. "How do we put this into practice?" they persistently ask. We owe the most gratitude to them for their constant supply of new ideas and for continually requesting materials they can use.

We've always thought of The Five Practices of Exemplary Leadership® as both a process for planning change and as a set of skills for guiding change. To help people use The Five Practices as a guide to change, we initially wrote a ten-page list of probing questions that walked people step-by-step through a real-life initiative. That initial list of questions was then transformed into "The Next Personal-Best Planner" by our colleagues at The Tom Peters Company: Homi Eshaghi, Lynne Parode, Christy Tonge, and Cathy Weselby.

When it came time to completely revise the original text and create *The Leadership Challenge Workbook* in 2003, we were blessed with the talents of Janis Chan. This latest revision benefits enormously from the work of our trusted friend and gifted writer Leslie Stephen.

An extremely supportive, encouraging, and skilled group of professionals at Jossey-Bass and Pfeiffer have worked with us on this new edition, as well as on previous editions. Lisa Shannon, Associate Publisher, convinced her colleagues that *The Leadership Challenge Workbook* was worthy of trade-book status, and she has been a constant champion, providing outstanding leadership in the expansion of our line of books, materials, and programs. We continue to be grateful for her confidence in us. Heartfelt thank-you's also go out to Marisa Kelley, acquiring editor on this revision, Kathleen Dolan Davies, director of Product Development and Customer Research, and Michael Kay, senior production editor, for their persistence in actually getting the book into shape for publication, and to Rebecca Taff for her skills in copyediting, proofing, and layout.

Finally, our thanks to every one of you who want to continue to pursue your leadership dreams and advance your personal skills. Never forget that you make a difference.

# About the Authors

**JIM KOUZES AND BARRY POSNER** have been working together for more than thirty years, studying leaders, researching leadership, conducting leadership development seminars, and being leaders themselves in various capacities. They are coauthors of the award-winning, best-selling book *The Leadership Challenge*. Since its first edition in 1987, *The Leadership Challenge* has sold over two million copies worldwide and is available in more than twenty-two languages. It has won numerous awards, including the Critics' Choice Award from the nation's book review editors and the James A. Hamilton Hospital Administrators' Book-of-the-Year Award, and was selected as one of the top ten books on leadership in *The Top 100 Business Books of All Time*.

Jim and Barry have coauthored more than a dozen other award-winning leadership books, including *Credibility: How Leaders Gain and Lose It, Why People Demand It*; *The Truth About Leadership: The No-Fads, Heart-of-the-Matter Facts You Need to Know*; *A Leader's Legacy*; *Encouraging the Heart*; *The Student Leadership Challenge*; and *The Academic Administrator's Guide to Exemplary Leadership*. They also developed the highly acclaimed *Leadership Practices Inventory* (LPI), a 360-degree questionnaire for assessing leadership behavior, which is one of the most widely used leadership assessment instruments in the world, along with the Student LPI. More than five hundred doctoral dissertations and academic research projects have been based on their The Five Practices of Exemplary Leadership® model.

Among the honors and awards that Jim and Barry have received are the American Society for Training and Development's (ASTD) highest award for their Distinguished Contribution to Workplace Learning and Performance; they have been named Management/Leadership Educators of the Year by the International Management Council; ranked by *Leadership*

*Excellence* magazine in the top twenty on its list of the Top 100 Thought Leaders; named among the Top 50 Leadership Coaches in the nation (according to *Coaching for Leadership*); and listed among *HR Magazine's* Most Influential International Thinkers.

Jim and Barry are frequent speakers, and each has conducted leadership development programs for hundreds of organizations, including Apple, Applied Materials, ARCO, AT&T, Australia Institute of Management, Australia Post, Bank of America, Bose, Charles Schwab, Cisco Systems, Clorox, Community Leadership Association, Conference Board of Canada, Consumers Energy, Deloitte Touche, Dorothy Wylie Nursing Leadership Institute, Dow Chemical, Egon Zehnder International, Federal Express, Genentech, Google, Gymboree, HP, IBM, Jobs DR-Singapore, Johnson & Johnson, Kaiser Foundation Health Plans and Hospitals, Intel, Itau Unibanco, L.L. Bean, Lawrence Livermore National Labs, Lucile Packard Children's Hospital, Merck, Motorola, NetApp, Northrop Grumman, Novartis, Oakwood Temporary Housing, Oracle, Petronas, Roche Bioscience, Siemens, 3M, Toyota, the U.S. Postal Service, United Way, USAA, Verizon, VISA, Westpac, and The Walt Disney Company. They have lectured at more than sixty college and university campuses.

**JIM KOUZES** is the Dean's Executive Fellow of Leadership, Leavey School of Business, at Santa Clara University, and lectures on leadership around the world to corporations, governments, and non-profits. He is a highly regarded leadership scholar, an experienced executive, and the *Wall Street Journal* cited him as one of the twelve best executive educators in the United States. In 2010, Jim received the Thought Leadership Award from the Instructional Systems Association, the most prestigious award given by the trade association of training and development industry providers. He was listed as one of *HR Magazine's* Most Influential International Thinkers for 2010 and 2011, named one of the 2010 and 2011 Top 100 Thought Leaders in Trustworthy Business Behavior by *Trust Across America,* and ranked by *Leadership Excellence* magazine as number sixteen on its list of the Top 100 Thought Leaders. In 2006 Jim was presented with the Golden Gavel, the highest honor awarded by Toastmasters International. Jim served as president, CEO, and chairman of The Tom Peters Company from 1988 through 1999, and prior to that led the Executive Development Center at Santa Clara University (1981 to 1987). Jim founded the Joint Center for Human Services Development at San Jose State University (1972 to 1980) and was on the staff of the School of Social Work, University of Texas. His career in training and development began in 1969 when he conducted seminars for Community Action Agency staff and volunteers in the war on poverty. Following graduation from Michigan State University (B.A. degree with honors in political science), he served as a Peace Corps volunteer (1967 to 1969). Jim can be reached at jim@kouzes.com.

**BARRY POSNER** is Accolti Professor of Leadership at the Leavey School of Business, Santa Clara University, where he served as Associate Dean for Graduate Education, Associate Dean for Executive Education and Dean of the School for twelve years (1997 to 2009). He has been a distinguished visiting professor at Hong Kong University of Science and Technology, Sabanci University (Istanbul), and the University of Western Australia. At Santa Clara he has received the President's Distinguished Faculty Award, the school's Extraordinary Faculty Award, and several other outstanding teaching and academic honors. An internationally renowned scholar and educator, Barry is author or coauthor of more than one hundred research and practitioner-focused articles. He currently serves on the editorial review boards for *Leadership and Organization Development* and *The International Journal of Servant-Leadership.* In 2011 he received the Outstanding Scholar Award for Career Achievement from the *Journal of Management Inquiry.*

Barry received his baccalaureate degree with honors in political science from the University of California, Santa Barbara, his master's degree in public administration from The Ohio State University, and his doctoral degree in organizational behavior and administrative theory from the University of Massachusetts, Amherst. Having consulted with a wide variety of public- and private-sector organizations around the globe, Barry also works at a strategic level with a number of community-based and professional organizations, currently sitting on the board of directors of EMQ FamiliesFirst. He has served previously on the board of the American Institute of Architects (AIA), Big Brothers/Big Sisters of Santa Clara County, Center for Excellence in Nonprofits, Junior Achievement of Silicon Valley and Monterey Bay, Public Allies, San Jose Repertory Theater, Sigma Phi Epsilon Fraternity, and several start-up companies. Barry can be reached at bposner@scu.edu.

## Notes

# Are you ready to make leading a daily practice?

Enhance Your Workbook Experience by Downloading **The Leadership Challenge Mobile Tool**—now available in the iTunes store!

For leaders of all ages and all levels of experience, this app includes several practical features that serious leaders will find useful on a daily basis, including:

- A seamless request-and-receive feedback process through which overall leadership performance can be tracked and measured.
- Helpful practice routines that can easily integrate into your work as a leader.
- A concise overview of The Leadership Challenge model—The Five Practices of Exemplary Leadership® and accompanying real leader cases that can be shared with friends and colleagues.
- Brief author videos that provide the opportunity to see Jim Kouzes and Barry Posner comment on their time-tested, evidence-based model.
- An inspirational Quote of the Day.
- A news feed with the latest leadership advice as well as updates on related events, products, and services.

### For pricing and other information, scan this code or visit pfeiffer.com/go/pfeifferapps